THE HOLLYWOOD PROFESSIONALS

Volume Two:

Henry King
Lewis Milestone
Sam Wood

by
Clive Denton
Kingsley Canham
Tony Thomas

This new series spotlights the work of the many professional directors at work in Hollywood during its heyday—talents who might otherwise be ignored by film students and historians. This volume contains monographs on, and very detailed filmographies of Henry King, Lewis Milestone, and Sam Wood, who between them made scores of familiar movies with a competence and a gloss now rarely seen in the cinema.

$4.95

Acknowledgements

The publishers would like to thank Kingsley Canham for his work in checking all the filmographies in this volume, and for his encouragement for the series as a whole. Stills by courtesy of Metropolitan Toronto Library Board, Chris Wicking, 20th Century-Fox, United Artists, John R. Lebold, Library of Academy of Motion Picture Arts and Sciences, M-G-M, RKO Radio Pictures, Paramount Pictures, Warner Bros., and the three authors of these essays.

Contents

way to the climactic scene high on a red-earthed Georgia hillside which at last justifies the title. Husband and wife are now in strong rapport. They have lived through sickness, prejudice, jealousy and their child's death. In spite of these things, or because of them, they are deeply in love. She offers to him the words of Ruth from the Old Testament: "Whither thou goest I will go, and where thou lodgest I will lodge, and thy people shall be my people, and thy God my God."

Perhaps King's greatest strength as a director is that constant ability to make us really believe that two people are in love. Hollywood romantic films have been common enough, heaven knows. How often, though, have the feeling and the emotion had to be taken on trust? In his work, there has been no doubt that Susan Hayward loved William Lundigan, that Nancy Kelly loved Tyrone Power, that Shirley Jones loved Gordon MacRae and that Jennifer Jones loved God. Typical also of the stories which, fortunately, he has been paid to put on film is the longevity of a romantic feeling, through tribulations and changing circumstances. Much of King's long career has been dedicated to an idealistic but not fatuous celebration of chivalry and a form of romance as much akin to friendship as to passion. Is this approach "sentimental"? It is, I think, an *honest* sentiment, almost never sugary and committed to a human affirmation not easily achieved nor maintained in any facile manner.

Although Henry King has made several more ambitious films, *I'd Climb the Highest Mountain* is fully characteristic of the man. Superbly shot in colour on location, well paced and adroitly modulated, it is a lyrical saga of ordinary people, each viewed by the director as extraordinary, because unique and personal to him. The friendly "near neighbour" (Ruth Donnelly), the sanctimonious establishment man (Gene Lockhart), the adulterous Mrs. Billywith from Atlanta (Lynn Bari), the doubting intellectual (Alexander

Knox), the handsome sheep-less-black-than-painted (Rory Calhoun)—these are sketched in throughout this wonderfully informal
movie with a sure hand and a sense of humour. All the personal
touches in the film would be proven to me by time as consistent
and meaningful to the "Gentleman from Virginia" whose name
on a credit I always looked for from that time forward. The interest
and affection begun in me on that hot August afternoon have led
me to a study of Henry King's films, new and old, over the twenty
years since.

"You ask whether I consider myself a creator of Americana?
Can only say that I love Americana and do not feel we have to
create it. It is already here—but I do like to interpret it for the
screen."

This simple statement from the director of so many fine evocations
of American social history is at once revealing and, by its modesty,
inadequate. The essential point is that, for him, all the force bottled
up in that potent word "Americana" exists—to mix a watery meta-
phor, as a well-spring of inspiration. What he fails to mention is
the work and thought and instinct necessary to fill the screen with
a pioneer sentiment and spirit. Attempted Americana by many
routine directors contrasts, in its flatness, with the rich wealth of
atmosphere and meaning found pre-eminently in the cinema of
D. W. Griffith, John Ford—and Henry King. It is often a matter
of small things, of details germane to a total artistic vision. There
is, for example, a moment in King's memorable *Jesse James* (1939),
when word of the outlaw Jesse is sought from a farm woman
outside her Missouri homestead. She is hoeing the soil; careworn
and tired, she stands in a cheap cotton frock and floppy straw
hat to ward off the sun, like the eternal working woman of frontier
American history. The image is, in a way, nothing. You could go
off for popcorn and never see the lady, without losing the thread
of the plot. Yet the image is also everything. And it exists on two

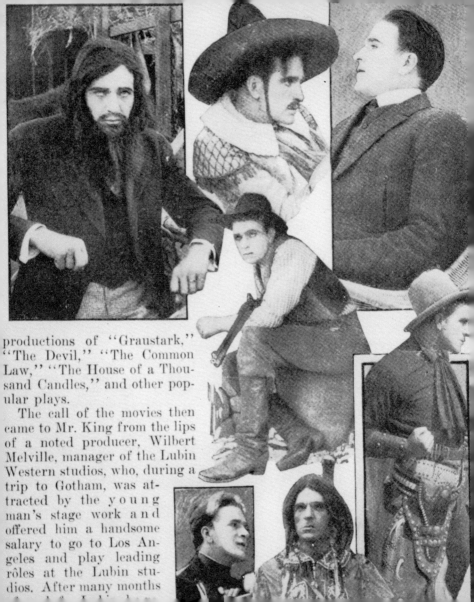

productions of "Graustark," "The Devil," "The Common Law," "The House of a Thousand Candles," and other popular plays.

The call of the movies then came to Mr. King from the lips of a noted producer, Wilbert Melville, manager of the Lubin Western studios, who, during a trip to Gotham, was attracted by the young man's stage work and offered him a handsome salary to go to Los Angeles and play leading rôles at the Lubin studios. After many months adventure. Nineteen-fourteen films in which he is listed include *A Will o'the Wisp* and *The Moth and the Flame.* He began to direct in 1915, usually also acting in his own films (which would be of short or medium length). Some of his many titles in 1917 reflect that period's heavy reliance on simple melodrama tempered with sentiment. They include *Sunshine and Gold, Souls in Pawn, The Bride's Silence, The Unafraid, Southern Pride* and *Told at Twilight—* the last title being an astonishing signpost to his future mature career when many of his most potent and touching scenes would indeed happen in the half-light of evening hours. His co-stars in those early years ranged from Ruth Roland, the serial star, to Baby Marie Osborne, a juvenile whom he is said to have discovered (whether under a bush or in some bullrushes is not clear). He appeared opposite (and directed) the energetic and danger-prone Miss Roland in a 1915 Pathé serial enquiringly entitled *Who Pays?* I am reduced to guessing at Baby Marie's credits, apart from *Joy and the Dragon,* but *Twin Kiddies* also seems a safe bet. In the following years King, like his colleagues John Ford and Raoul Walsh, turned more and more from acting to directing only. His last performance co-starred him with Blanche Sweet in *Help Wanted —Male* (1920), but in the next two years columnists were still speculating that he would return to the screen. They were invariably lady columnists. One of them reported in 1922 that he would like to return to acting because all he enjoyed directing were fight scenes—a questionable statement ascribed to such a gentle and peaceable artist. Perhaps he was merely telling the lady what she wished to hear, for no more screen performances were forthcoming.

In directing, his mass of early experience was increased by a string of pictures featuring the Western star, William Russell, in 1918/19. Then came the first King film to win wide popular success

Opposite: King featured in his roles for the Balboa Company (from "Motion Picture Magazine," February 1915)

King directed Norma Talmadge in *The Woman Disputed* (1928), with music and effects on the track, and Eleanor Boardman in *She Goes to War* (1929), a partial "talkie." Norma's vehicle starred her as a prostitute—good-hearted, of course—in a variation of the "Boule de Suif" story which has since become so dear to the cinema's collective heart, contributing to the plots of Ford's *Stagecoach* (1939) and Robert Wise's *Mademoiselle Fifi* (1944). Eleanor Boardman, for her part, went off to fight, disguised as a boy.

Very few of King's films up to the period we have now reached are (to understate the case) readily available for viewing today. There are yawning gaps in almost everybody's knowledge of King's silent pictures that make him, as Andrew Sarris has decreed, a "Subject for Further Research." It is probably significant that the films which have been preserved and are often revived benefit from engrossing stories and strong human situations, honestly depicted, at least against the standards and conventions of the time. *Tol'able David, The White Sister* and *Stella Dallas* may require slight critical indulgence here and there at this date, because time has dulled their sheen a little and laid bare some contrivances of plot. But such indulgence need be very slight, because of King's transparently sincere involvement with his people and his places. His best sound films are similarly endowed with qualities of good scripting and basic human importance. He has never been a "between the lines" director (like Douglas Sirk or Vincente Minnelli); not for King any great incentive from the tension which may exist between a film-maker and his material. His work, on the contrary, is largely free from tension, either nervous or artistic, and so needs to relate closely to open aspects of plot and subject. When such relation is absent, then a film of only passing interest emerges from King. And in even his finest films, his direction uplifts a story, illuminates it, rather than changing it to something different. King can be subtle—infinitely so—but never oblique. *She Goes to*

War and two films made the following year, 1930 (*Hell Harbor* and *Eyes of the World*), were again Inspiration Pictures, the company's active work having been continued in the mid-Twenties by Barthelmess, with various other directors, such as John S. Robertson for *The Bright Shawl* (1923) which, like *Tol'able David*, was adapted from a Joseph Hergesheimer story and scripted by Edmund Goulding. Unfortunately, it seems that around 1929 King's inspiration was temporarily lacking. It is very doubtful that these last three Inspiration Pictures ever transcended the triteness suggested by their synopses. Certainly they made little mark in those early

Richard Barthelmess in TOL'ABLE DAVID: the boy,
the girl, and the landscape

of poor Stella, deliberately over-ate in order to add some pounds to her figure. The information is conveyed in fan magazines of the time, one of which also ordered its readers to see this film or forever hold their peace about the art of the motion picture! Stella has given up her daughter, for the girl's own sake, to be educated as a young lady. As a result, the girl is rising in the social world to which her humble mother cannot belong. Her daughter is shown with a group of rich friends—beautiful young Twenties people—idyllically happy among a setting of smooth lawns and verdant foliage. Suddenly her mother sails into view, lovingly but tactlessly seeking her out. The daughter, horrified, shrinks back and tried to hide, while her friends start murmuring. Who is that funny woman? The audience, split between feelings of sympathy for both mother and daughter, now takes the onslaught of an intermingling of medium and close shots. The fat and ageing Stella, dressed ridiculously in a hideous striped costume, advances over the grass towards the young group. As she walks, the medium view is dissolved into a much closer one, with quite extraordinary impact. It is a bravura impact born of discretion beforehand. Henry King learned early the value of *relative* abandon within what might almost be called, in a modern phrase, "minimal cinema."

As one of Hollywood's supreme craftsmen, he also learned and appreciated the actual pictorial sheen and loveliness possible with star portraiture within his silent movies. He and his cameramen produced breathtaking likenesses of Lillian Gish and Vilma Banky, later equalled (in other hands) only by close shots of Garbo and Dietrich. This understanding of portrait heads within a film became a rapidly waning art in the sound era but the knowledge remained with Henry King. He saved some of his loveliest and most moving shots of this nature for Susan Hayward in the Fifties. The stunning Miss Hayward, of the shining eyes and flaming hair, proved a more than fitting subject for such innocent cunning and devotion. Susan, in *David and Bathsheba,* against a mass of orchard blossom; Susan, in *Untamed,* carrying a lamp down the sweeping staircase of an Irish mansion; such images stay in the mind and form a tribute both to present beauty and to past technique.

★   ★   ★

Dorothy Gish and William Powell in ROMOLA

Alice Faye and Don Ameche in ALEXANDER'S RAGTIME BAND

of mass movement made *Alexander's Ragtime Band* the best of this 20th Century-Fox *genre.*

Strangely enough, the old and the new Fox did share one common denominator. This was a tendency towards Americana. William Fox, in his *régime,* gave John Ford his first major opportunity with *The Iron Horse* and the success in 1924 of this railroad-building saga turned Fox's factory to all kinds of American dreams and memories in silent pictures, including the strange tangents of Tom Mix's modernised westerns and the hauntingly Americanised nameless landscape and city of F. W. Murnau's unforgettable *Sunrise* (1928). Americana fitted Henry King's hand like a glove and with this glove he handled the fires of inspiration, producing for the old Fox Corporation his first sound masterpiece, the original *State Fair* (1933). Under Zanuck, however, Americana looked at first a less likely prospect. When D.F.Z. had controlled Warners' production in the early Thirties, gangsters and gold diggers were more in evidence than conjured pictures of a pioneering land. Nor had his own Twentieth Century movies inclined in that direction. His feelings about the Farmer perpetually Taking a Wife must have seemed ready to clinch the matter in 1935. Remarkably enough, a latent affinity with Americana was somewhere deep in Zanuck all along. King *did* prosper with it, at 20th Century-Fox, as did John Ford in 1939 with *Young Mr. Lincoln* and *Drums along the Mohawk*. It is highly likely that his employment of these two giants of American historic sentiment started Zanuck on a path he might not otherwise have taken. For whatever reason, it became a well-trodden path at his studio, involving in later years such diverse and foreign-born directors as Otto Preminger (*Centennial Summer, River of No Return*) and Jacques Tourneur (*Way of a Gaucho*). Zanuck even re-made *The Farmer Takes a Wife*—many times figuratively and once literally, as a frame for Betty Grable's talents, directed by Henry Levin, with songs and Technicolor, in 1953. There would seem little doubt, then, that the chance to make pictures with subjects amenable to him partly accounts for King's uniquely lengthy tenure with 20th Century-Fox. Whatever other reasons there may be, among them are surely two implicit tributes. One salute must go to the studio's high production standards and readiness to spend money to make money, in proportion to the potential of major projects. The second salute goes even more directly to the qualities as a leader and something of a prophet of that much discussed, sometimes maligned but ultimately respected film industry titan, Darryl F. Zanuck. Other writers have given

The producer's forward thrust and the director's skill and sympathy met, in both these films, on an equal and appropriate footing. *The Gunfighter*, especially, can be seen as a producer's concept. Spare, lean, an anticipatory *High Noon*, even to the pendulum swinging on the clock, to an extent which would have had to be noticed by Kramer's critics two years later, did not film reviewers have such notoriously short memories. (There is even action under the credit titles, as Peck rides to the small town where Richard Jaeckel's punk hooligan forces a confrontation.) Naturally, the King talents are readily apparent in both films. They are simply not his most personal good movies, that is all. I do not grudge him praise but I hope one day more cinephiles will like and respect Henry King for what he essentially is.

The Henry King hero or heroine is lonely. Many of his leading characters share, as a common bond, some form of isolation from their fellow men. Sometimes this isolation is physical and may spring from the conditions of a life outside the law. Frank and Jesse, the hounded outlaw brothers in *Jesse James*, fall into this fearful category, as do Gregory Peck's reluctant killer who gives *The Gunfighter* its title and the same actor's vengeful husband in *The Bravados*, seeking his wife's murderers but pardoning the last in a moment of human understanding. More essentially, however, the isolation is of the spirit and, ironically, usually involves the ideal of service to a community. Peck again is the Air Force officer in *Twelve O'Clock High*, whose feelings of responsibility to his men and his position tire him into a breakdown, when he can no longer "climb into the cockpit." This stress of service is no respecter of rank or person. Jean Hersholt's *Country Doctor* experiences it, as does *Wilson*, the President of the United States. In King's vision, there are compensations and consolations for all sacrifice. His world is a generous place in which spiritual ache is relieved by love, friendship and, to some extent, sheer bustle. What we may term "King Country" has a lot of *people* in it. A weary protagonist can expect to be cheered by kind words from a supporting player or distracted from his own problems by the diversity and simple *interest* of life around him. Still, the loneliness remains a central theme. It presses hard on those whose service takes religious forms. (King became a Catholic some time after *The White Sister's* production.) The circuit riding minister and his wife find some ignorance and suspicion mixed with their generally warm welcome into the Georgia hills. In *The Song of Bernadette* (a film of very restrained sentiment, incidentally, which many sceptical people like better than they expect to) Bernadette Soubirous is tormented by questions and jealousies and doubts after she has seen The Virgin Mary in a vision. And Lillian Gish becomes a nun in *The White Sister*.

There are many parallels between this film and *The Song of Bernadette*. Although twenty years separate them, the visual continuity in scenes of convent life is a remarkable gift from one picture to the other (and both may have influenced Fred Zinnemann with *The Nun's Story*). This is a context where the extreme visual blacks and whites contrast with an emotional tone of ambivalent grey. *The White Sister* relies unusually heavily for King on atmosphere and nuance. A young woman of high family (Gish) falls deeply in love with a handsome and dashing suitor (Ronald Colman). Believing him killed in the World War, she enters a convent as a novice and eventually becomes the gracious lady of the title. It transpires that Colman was captured in the war, not killed. He returns and tries to persuade Gish to renounce her vows. She refuses but is wavering when a natural disaster (the eruption of Mount Vesuvius) delays a romantic decision. Colman dies heroically

might be the last people in the world," muses Margie (for that, charmingly, is the girl's name, in the year when a future Margie, Jeanne Crain, is only eight years old). But they are not the last people in the world. In the morning they arrive at the fair where, among the bustling crowds, Gaynor finds lasting love (with Lew Ayres) and Foster has a more fleeting but educative fling with a friendly floozie (Sally Eilers). Technically, the fair is represented partly by sets, partly by background scenes taken by King and Hal Mohr at an actual state fair in the film's pre-production period. The matching of these latter views with foreground action is obvious enough to the experienced eye. But director and photographer have made good use of them, suggesting action by frequent tracking shots, as in Foster's long walk through the grounds, in front of tents, animal pens, the midway. And our visual expectations, having adjusted to this context, are likely to be quietly exploded. Knowing that Foster is in foreground against a pre-filmed background, it is a mild surprise to see men with ropes and hammers come into frame briefly, during the track, *in front of* Foster. Since there is now a growing awareness of cinematographers' work in its own right, one should say in fairness that parts of *State Fair* bear the stamp of Hal Mohr's genius for lighting and angling, in particular the night scenes of bizarre amusement rides on the midway. A high-diving act immediately recalls Mohr's fine work with similar carnival pictures in Michael Curtiz's silent melodrama, *The Third Degree* (1927).

Both parents win honours in the fair's competitions, Rogers with Blue Boy, Dresser with her pickles (which have been liberally bolstered by apple brandy). King's flair with actors is apparent in the pickle-tasting scene, one of the few openly comic sequences in all his work, yet still in perfect tune with the rest of the film and a million miles from caricature. The experts strut and gargle and taste, each small-part player registering delightfully for his

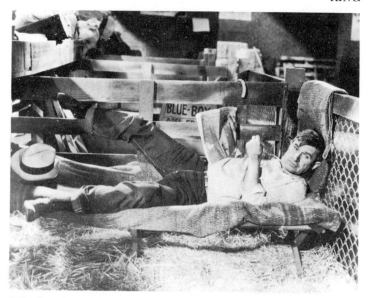

"The best State Fair in our State": Will Rogers

brief moment in the limelight. Dresser, in suspense before her prizes are announced, fans herself gradually more agitatedly until she is almost flailing the air around her. It is perhaps surprising that such simple elements in *State Fair* add up to such a charming, complete picture of a way of life vanishing even as it was recorded. In the later musical versions of this novel, the slight story became merely a peg for songs, colourful settings, assorted romances and more songs. Strangely enough, with this hindsight, King's *State Fair* is full of cues for music. Indeed there is music but no direct character singing. Janet Gaynor puts on a record, Will Rogers

33

turns on the car radio, an off-screen chorus sings a featured tune as Gaynor and Ayres ride one of Mohr's picturesque flying machines. Incidentally, William K. Everson asserts that this song was shortened on the reissue print I recently saw (reissued, that is, soon after Rogers's death, with the 20th Century-Fox trademark). Elsewhere in this version, it is now less explicit that Foster has spent a whole night with Eilers. While on this interesting subject, it is possible to conjecture that sweet Margie might have dallied beyond a crucial point with *her* handsome beau. They lie back on a mossy bank with a kiss of unusual intensity (unusual, anyway, for such a movie). But there's nothing to worry mom. Both son and daughter sit with her next morning watching the triumph of Blue Boy, as though no butter would melt in their rustic mouths.

The film ends touchingly. Back home again, the family sits on the front porch. It begins to rain. There is small talk. Margie hears a car approaching and, on impulse, runs to the front gate. It *is* her fairground *fiancée*, whom she had almost in caution rejected. The rain soaks them but they are, in spirit, singing in it. *State Fair* has something of a musical's *joie de vivre*, without the need for music. Behind the embracing couple is a huge billboard, still advertising the just-ended fair. The sheets of rain wash off the poster. Underneath is written THE END. This is not *quite* an alienation device; it just keeps the movie in perspective.

Jesse James was King's second film in the new "perfected" Technicolor and his fourth film starring the young Tyrone Power. Both facts illustrate his prestige in Hollywood, for colour was the current (and expensive) fad and Power had been successfully nurtured, by Zanuck, as Fox's major star. In 1939, our "flying director" was flying high. Though prestige cannot guarantee quality,

JESSE JAMES: "They were drove to it."

happily *Jesse James* is one of King's finest films and my personal favourite. It possesses a magnificent forward-pressing attack, a surge of images, not always present in his work, together with those moments of calm and reflection that are native to him.

As the film's credits suggest, much historical research was conducted for Nunnally Johnson's screenplay. One may assume that, however greatly this contributed to the film's unusually strong sense of time and place, it did not inhibit a fairly free interpretation of the James Brothers' motives and methods. An old lady, living in the James's area of Missouri, was once asked by a friend of mine whether the outlaws had truly been noble or heroic figures. She replied that they were not. Jesse and Frank were much less appealing in her memory than Power and Henry Fonda made them on the screen. They had been cruel, mean, spiteful, provocative of trouble. Then the lady paused in her denunciation and in a few words summed up many years of accumulated legend: "Of course, they was drove to it!" This is very much the film's viewpoint, ignoring the brothers' adolescent plundering with Quantrill's Raiders. Here, they are peaceable farm boys, driven to crime by unscrupulous officials of the advancing railroad (including Brian

Tyrone Power and Nancy Kelly in JESSE JAMES

Donlevy, typically and robustly villainous and Donald Meek, untypically and sneakily so). Their later outlaw careers take in train robberies and bank hold-ups, before Jesse, now living a quiet pseudonymous life, is shot down by a former colleague: to quote his tombstone, "a traitor whose name is not worthy to be mentioned here."

Whatever distortions of history it contains, *Jesse James* manages to be both a stirring adventure (in its earlier stages), and, finally, a moving study of notoriety unable to turn peaceable and live unmolested. The closing scenes look forward to Gregory Peck's similar troubled last days as *The Gunfighter*. Peck there is still an idealised figure, not much corrupted by violence, although the latter film has an "adult" reputation which *Jesse James* does not. Perhaps the body of the 1939 film is too exciting, too energetic for that sort of critical attention. It is worth remarking that never can horses have been so thoroughly used as (literally) carriers of action (symbolically), agents of movement. They crash through plate-glass windows, ride tumultuously over the terrain and even plunge over a cliff into the river, as Frank and Jesse make a particularly daring escape. A word of reassurance should be added for animal lovers who have criticised this breathtaking moment. A quick and scarcely perceptible cut just before the plunge suggests that simulated animals actually took the fall.

In 1958, King made another splendid Western melodrama, *The Bravados*—the last film, I think, to be fully worthy of his talent. It has several parallels with *Jesse James*, most especially a brilliantly filmed jail-break sequence at twilight whose concentrated atmosphere is in debt to the 1939 forerunner. In some quarters, *The Bravados* has been called, most inaccurately, a "neurotic Western." In fact, its admittedly bloody story has an almost Elizabethan dramatic purity, stressing the brutalising effect of revengeful violence upon the revenger. A real neurotic Western, in 1957, was

Nicholas Ray's re-make of *Jesse James*, now entitled *The True Story of Jesse James*. What is truth? Since the studio was still disinclined to paint Jesse very black, the re-worked script now played up the violence inflicted on the James family and lugubriously extended Johnson's previously succinct writing of Jesse as a human force with potential for both good and evil. There is, to be fair, a touch at the close of Ray's film which I could wish King had put in his original. After Jesse's murder, small crowds gather in his homestead and souvenir hunters begin to steal the family mementoes. This well represents the moment when the firm edges of history begin to melt into the soft entanglements of legend. In all respects but this, the legendary quality of Jesse James is much better expressed in Henry King's spirited, big but unpretentious film of 1939.

Twelve O'Clock High contains probably the finest opening scenes of any King film. One aspect of them is derivative in conception but first-rate in execution. It is established (very briefly and economically) that Dean Jagger is an American in London, 1949. He decides to make a return visit to the site of the American air base at "Archbury," somewhere in the English countryside, where he had been stationed during the war. We do not yet know the reason for his sentimental journey, however, as he arrives at a small railway station and makes his way along a country lane and through a field of waving wheat. Ostensibly, this arcadian landscape represents England's rural areas. The actual location is American, though, and to anyone familiar with King's work is redolent of a long line of previously recorded lanes and fields. Its natural beauty—lovingly framed and angled—underlines the tugging nostalgia (yes, again) of Jagger's return visit. The same

Shifting authority: Gregory Peck and Gary Merrill in
TWELVE O'CLOCK HIGH

beauty, with its sense of natural peace and eternal regeneration, serves effectively, if subliminally, as a symbol of life and a needed memorial to the dead.

For now, the mood changes, with a superbly placed chord of Alfred Newman's music. Jagger has suddenly reached the runway of his old air force unit. The tarmac lies, now rutted and wasting, like a scar almost hidden by the new tissue of the country scene. The idea of an empty airfield revisited and recalled from the war derives from Anthony Asquith's *The Way to the Stars* (Britain, 1945). As Jagger walks over its surface, he hears in his memory faint echoes of the songs once sung there by young off-duty voices. "Don't Sit under the Apple Tree," "Bless 'Em All," "We're Poor Little Lambs Who Have Lost Our Way." And then the first remembered sounds of a plane, revving up for take-off. The impact of sound and picture is here intense and perfectly judged; two years later, King is to do similarly, in a different context, with the ghostly sounds of battle—heard but not seen—recalled in the mind of Biblical King David.

The noise of planes gives way to the sight of them, so subtly as to defeat recognition of the exact moment of transition. The time is now 1943, a hectic period of American involvement in bombing missions over Germany. The men are exhausted and resentful; their commander (Gary Merrill) is worried and weary to the point of breakdown. He will soon be replaced. It is night. Some of the flyers are returning (only some *do* return) from a mission. King and Leon Shamroy present a run of short, staccato scenes, with the men caught by the camera in tight groupings and angled, claustrophobic close shots. This is King on different ground and in uncharacteristic mood, but functioning superbly. Later, as the story unfolds and the film's tension can be reduced, he finds more space within his settings of offices, assembly rooms and hangars. In fact, deep-focus compositions and certain groupings of men spaced across the width of a room *deliberately* loosen the tautness which the opening has possessed and which is then saved for a few crucial moments. If, as suggested earlier, Zanuck is calling the tune on this production—King has the band parts.

Twelve O'Clock High brought King his best critical notices for years and was immensely popular with the public. This double-barrelled success must be seen in the context of the time. Films even equivocally critical of war and warfare are rare in an immediate postwar period. By 1949 it was possible—but still unexpected—for a big commercial film like this to question the validity of pushing young men harder and harder into intense, "sophisticated" battle. Paul Stewart's sympathetic doctor speaks of the requests he gets for sick leave and relief from duty. "How much can a man take?" he asks. "What's physical and what isn't?" This was still an awkward question after the Korean war and Hollywood could still be considered rather daring to put it, in films like *The Rack* (1956) and *Time Limit* (1957). Films feed on films and wars, unhappily, seem to feed on wars. Seen again today, *Twelve O'Clock High* is less impressive than contemporary reviews suggest on the grounds of either innovation or thematic courage. It derives from a number of sources (both versions of *The Dawn Patrol* not excluded), of which Sam Wood's *Command Decision* (1948) is the most immediate in time and emphasis—the latter being the solitude of authority and the pain but necessity of leadership decisions. Further, *Twelve O'Clock High* does not really commit itself to any radical stand. That war is a bloody shame and leaders are dedicated but fallible—this is the extent of its non-conformity. However, the script's caution and equivocation are considerably modified by King's fine handling of his action and actors, especially actors (even Hugh Marlowe seems interested). Remembering that King needs a good script to start his adrenalin pumping, it is only fair to say that this *is* a good script, although slightly repetitive, in terms of dramatic clarity and character delineation. Given this, King's sense of discretion and what can only be termed "fair play" redeem the film's basic uncertainty of attitude and turn it towards a Shavian ambiguity, with equal time and fair weight given to all opinions. At the end of a Shaw play, the audience has heard many ideas, many voices. If one turn of thought stays with them, it is because the author has drawn it from them, through some human (and humane) recognition. He has not planted it there. As Shaw with words, so King with images. The character of General Frank Savage receives, through camera placement and lighting and pictorial context, King's commendation, compassion and respect. In the role of this tough, rigid, self-doubting but self-dominating authoritarian, Gregory Peck is seen often alone, either contemplating or thinking back on a "command decision." He even takes pains to keep a momentary satisfaction to himself, turning his briefly smiling face away from the men. In group scenes, he is often physically at a distance from other actors. He is very much alone one misty morning when—a temporary breakdown ironically imminent because of strain on him, the disciplinarian—he can no longer swing into the cockpit of his plane.

Frank Savage is *such* a solitary figure among King's lonely heroes that we do not know what happens to him after the war's (and before the picture's) ending. The film closes, as it opened, on the figure played by Dean Jagger—played so well, incidentally, that he deservedly won an Academy Award. A quiet, contemplative man, temperamentally suited more to the comradeship than the practice of war, who had sometimes sided with military exigency but grudgingly, sadly. Jagger is walking back to the railway station as the final credit appears. The English-cum-American landscape has been made only temporarily safe for democracy. It is a bitter-sweet ending, especially with hindsight to question such things as bombing in Vietnam, whether the pilots are under pressure or not. And Jagger is a strangely lonely figure too. But the positive, the heart-warming thing is this. King has made his personal evaluation of the men in his story. We may agree or not, as we wish. Nobody is totally shrugged off or dismissed. Peck's martinet has gained King's understanding and partial acceptance. Jagger has gained his affection and love.

This may be as good a place as any to question some assertions made in recent reminiscences by Hollywood photographers, as to who was finally responsible for what. After Leon Shamroy had shot *Twelve O'Clock High,* King next worked with Arthur Miller on *The Gunfighter*. Both films make extensive use of the deep-focus and wide-view photography already mentioned, especially for dramatic isolation of a central character (Peck in each case). Did the two cinematographers have a chat in the studio restaurant—or is it possible that King knows something about visuals, after all?

In 1953, when all Hollywood was suffering from dwindling audiences and falling receipts, 20th Century-Fox announced a policy decision. Beginning with *The Robe*, all the studio's major productions would henceforth be made in CinemaScope, an anamorphic wide-screen process with an approximate ratio of 2½ (width) to one (height). The Fox publicity machine ground out some treasurable press releases, referring to what was grandiloquently termed "The Miracle Mirror Screen." The world learned that "CinemaScope stuns with its glory as it embraces the audience without the use of glasses." The latter part of this confident statement contained a swift kick at three-dimensional films, which were then being offered in Hollywood, somewhat tentatively, as a panacea for economic ills and the masses' fickle flight away from the cinemas towards cars, washing machines and the washing machine's lookalike, television. In an industry frantically hedging its bets and looking simultaneously in all directions for salvation, Fox's decision was courageous. Whether it was sensible is another matter. There was great uncertainty about the merits of Cinema-Scope, both from concerned filmgoers and from Hollywood craftsmen. The deficiencies of early CinemaScope lenses have been recalled by ace cinematographer Leon Shamroy (who in 1953 was fresh from photographing his ninth Henry King film, *The Snows of Kilimanjaro*). As to the shape of the screen, a critic wrote acidly that, in the history of art, the frieze had attained an honourable but limited position.

In addition to technical drawbacks, the first CinemaScope films at Fox were limited by their subjects. The studio was becoming hidebound, forgetting its experimental times in the Forties and harking back to the "entertainment only" policy of 1935–39, only with less panache and bravado to carry things along. It was rumoured that the first twelve CinemaScope productions were simply the next twelve properties on the studio's previous schedule. This was in conflict with industry statements about the necessity for "big" subjects suitable to wall-to-wall screening. In any event, the newly conservative, withdrawal nature of Zanuck's thinking at this period is evident. Henry Koster directed *The Robe;* his colleagues at Fox followed with even less promising material. King was given nothing better than a decaying namesake, *King of the Khyber Rifles.* This story of old army loyalty and derring-do had been none too fresh when John Ford filmed it as *The Black Watch* in 1929. Twenty-five years later it proved impossibly hoary and moth-eaten and did nothing to revive the sagging career of Tyrone Power, who had naturally lost much of the youthful freshness of *Jesse James* and should have been allowed more parts of maturity and seriousness, such as he had shown he could handle. (*The Razor's Edge* (1946) and *Nightmare Alley* (1947), with Power in top gear, were both directed at Fox by Edmund Goulding, King's writer and assistant from the old Inspiration Pictures days.) Nor did King's subjects improve to any extent until, very happily for him and us, he was chosen to direct his first really sizable project in several years, the filming of Rodgers and Hammerstein's *Carousel.* Size, of course, is not everything but in this case a good thing came in a big package—and with technical improvements promoted under a new label, CinemaScope 55.

Actually, the shape of CinemaScope, with what at first seemed acres of screen and a new shock value given even to fairly innocuous cutting from set-up to set-up, did not disturb King from the start.

He replied to a "Sight and Sound" questionnaire about the process in glowing terms as to its potential for reviving the industry. The statement may be taken with several grains of salt, partly because of his close association with the studio now backing 'Scope with all its corporate might, partly on account of his Virginian disinclination to say anything bad about anything or anybody. Nevertheless, we need not presume him to have been unhappy about a screen ratio which encouraged his constant tendency to tell a story in pictures, with a lot of information contained within each composition and very little in the way of razzle-dazzle editing. Before *Carousel* his 'Scope movies suffered from poor subjects and scripts (though he himself might disagree about *Love Is a Many-Splendored Thing* which I believe is a personal favourite). They did not suffer from indecision or misjudgement about what to do with the bigger frame. It is true that, shortly after *Carousel*, the last two or three films of his long career do rather drag their feet. Whereas "measured" seems a fair description of most of his films' tempo, I would have to apply the word "static" to *Beloved Infidel* and *Tender Is The Night* (although neither is without true and delicate moments of acting and society depiction, so that they are certainly worthy of concluding a career which has had some honour in it). In any event, their lack of forward impetus would not seem to be caused merely by 'Scope.

My own fondness for *Carousel* must allow considerable credit to the original stage show and to Ferenc Molnar for providing, in his play "Liliom," the basis for a warm and touching fantasy which, in contrast to some people, I do *not* find excessively sentimental or sticky. The story centres on Billy, a fairground barker, and Julie, the young girl who loves him and marries him till death do them part but goes on loving him, through their daughter whom he has not seen until given leave from heaven for one day to visit the Maine Coast once more. Henry King has taken and played

Shirley Jones comforts the dying Gordon MacRae in CAROUSEL

fair by the stage show and added his, by this time long-accumu-
lated, feeling for tenderness, sense of place and atmosphere and
sincere involvement. Photographically, the major part of the film
is stunning. The fairground is Fox's first visual expanse really
suited to a CinemaScope panorama. There are still signs of technical
deficiencies. Sets sometimes merge badly with location shooting
and the colour—depending partly on which print one sees—is inclined to turn blue. All else is enchantment. Like so many King
couples before them, Shirley Jones and Gordon MacRae convince
us of a great and genuine love between them. The musical numbers and dramatic scenes are finely integrated. There is a grouping

around a country church which in itself justifies the invention of the cinema. At the end of the song, "When the Children Are Asleep," there is a view of sail boats on the evening ocean, brave and fragile against the red sky at night, which still lifts the heart. It is a twilight scene and the last small point I would like to emphasise is how often King's filmic day comes to a peak of quiet emotion at twilight time. That scene from *I'd Climb the Highest Mountain*, with which I began this essay and my experience of his films, happened at twilight too . . .

Gregory Peck and Susan Hayward in THE SNOWS OF KILIMANJARO

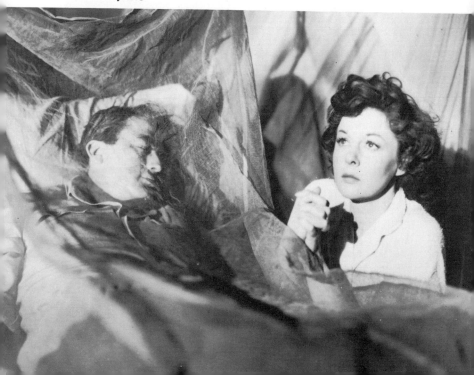

HENRY KING Filmography

In spite of many inquiries, it has not been possible to present, with reliable credits, a full listing of Henry King's early work as a director. The detailed filmography therefore is set out from early 1919 to 1961 only. The following is a partial list of short features directed by King from 1915 onwards.

WHO PAYS (15) serial, released in twelve three-reel episodes; THE BRAND OF MAN (15); JOY AND THE DRAGON (16); TWIN KIDDIES (17); THE CLIMBER (17); TOLD AT TWILIGHT (17); SUNSHINE AND GOLD (17); SOULS IN PAWN (17); THE BRIDE'S SILENCE (17); THE UNAFRAID (17); THE UPPER CRUST (17); SCEPTER OF SUSPICION (17); THE MAINSPRING (17); SOUTHERN PRIDE (17); A GAME OF WITS (17); MATE OF SALLY ANN (17); KING SOCIAL BRIARS (18); THE GHOST OF ROSY TAYLOR (18); BEAUTY AND THE ROGUE (18); POWERS THAT PRAY (18); THE LOCKED HEART (18).

During 1918 and 1919 King directed eleven films starring William Russell, mostly with western plots and settings. These were five or six reel features, produced by the American Film Company, with scenario credited to Stephen Fox. The titles are:—HEARTS OR DIAMONDS; UP ROMANCE ROAD; ALL THE WORLD TO NOTHING (copyright Oct. 18); HOBBS IN A HURRY (Oct. 18); WHEN A MAN RIDES ALONE (Dec. 18); WHERE THE WEST BEGINS (Feb. 19); BRASS BUTTONS (Apr. 19); SOME LIAR (Apr. 19); A SPORTING CHANCE (June 19); THIS HERO STUFF (July 19); SIX FEET FOUR (Sept. 19).

Following 23½ HOURS LEAVE (19), King directed H. B. Warner in seven films. The titles and dates are:—A FUGITIVE FROM MATRIMONY (19); HAUNTING SHADOWS (19); THE WHITE DOVE (20); UNCHARTED CHANNELS (20); ONE HOUR BEFORE DAWN (20); DICE OF DESTINY (20); WHEN WE WERE 21 (21).

The following complete listing from 1921 is prefaced by the ten earlier films on which some details are available.

BRASS BUTTONS (1919). Western farce in which the hero must clean up the town before he can marry the girl. *Sc:* Stephen Fox. *With:* William Russell, Eileen Percy, Helen Howard, Frank Brownlee, Bull Montana. *Prod:* American Film Co. 5r.

A SPORTING CHANCE (June 19). *With* William Russell (*John Stonehouse*), Fritzi Brunette (*Gilberte Bonheur*), George Periolat (*Edward Craig*), J. Farrell MacDonald (*Luther Ripley*), Lee Hill (*George Cornhill*), Perry Banks (*Aaron Witt*).

SIX FEET FOUR (Sept. 19). *With* William Russell (*Buck Thornton*), Charles French (*Henry Pollard*), Vola Vale (*Winifred Waverly*), Harvey Clark

(*Two-Handed Billy Comstock*), Clarence Burton (*Cole Dalton*), A. L. Garcia, Jack Collins, Calvert Carter, Perry Banks, John Carter.

23½ HOURS LEAVE (1919). Farce-comedy of army life, with a certain documentary value in depicting a "rookie" training camp of the First World War. *Sc:* Agnes C. Johnston (story by Mary Roberts Rinehart). *With* Douglas MacLean (*Sergeant Gray*), Doris Day (*Peggy Dodge*), Thomas Guise (*General Dodge*), Maxfield Stanley (*Table Sergeant*), Wade Boteler, Alfred Hollingsworth, Jack Nelson and N. Leinsky. *Prod:* Thomas H. Ince (Famous Players-Lasky). 5r. Re-made in 1937 (*Prod:* Douglas MacLean. *Dir:* John G. Blystone).

A FUGITIVE FROM MATRIMONY (1919). *With* H. B. Warner (*Stephen Van Courtlandt*), Seena Owen (*Barbara Riggs*), Adele Farrington (*Mrs. E. Elmer Riggs*), Walter Perry (*Zachariah E. Riggs*), Christine Mayo (*Edythe Arlington*), Matthew Biddulph, John Gough, Lulu Warrenton.

HAUNTING SHADOWS (1919). *Sc:* adapted from novel "The House of a Thousand Candles" by Meredith Nicholson. *With* H. B. Warner (*John Glenarm*), Edward Piel (*Arthur Pickering*), Charles Hill Mailes (*Bates*), Frank Lanning (*Morgan*), Florence Oberle (*Sister Theresa*), Marguerite Livingstone (*Marian Deveraux*). Previous version 1915 (*Prod:* Selig Polyscope Co.). Re-made in 1936 (*Dir:* Arthur Lubin). Both as THE HOUSE OF A THOUSAND CANDLES.

THE WHITE DOVE (1920). An idealist is shocked into the belief that all women are faithless, but changes his mind when he finds his mother left her husband for *his* father. *With* H. B. Warner (*Sylvester Lanyon*), James O. Barrows (*Matthew Lanyon*), Clare Adams (*Ella De Fries*), Herbert Greenwood (*Ebenezer Usher*), Donald McDonald (*Roderick Usher*), Virginia Lee Corbin, Ruth Renick.

UNCHARTED CHANNELS (1920). A rich man cuts off his son with a shilling. The son takes a job as a factory worker in the business he should have owned, and finds it in the hands of a shiftless uncle. A rich girl aids his efforts to take over the business and expose the labour racketeering. *With* H. B. Warner (*Timothy Webb, Jr.*), Kathryn Adams (*Sylvia Kingston*), Sam de Grasse (*Nicholas Schonn*), Evelyn Selby (*Elsa Smolski*), William Elmer (*Jim Baker*), Percy Challenger, Thomas H. Persse, J. P. Lockney.

ONE HOUR BEFORE DAWN (1920). Murder mystery, raising the question of whether a man can go against his nature under hypnosis. *Sc:* Frank Leon Smith (novel "Behind Red Curtains" by Mansfield Scott). *With* H. B. Warner (*George Clayton*), Anna Q. Nilsson (*Ellen Aldrich*), Frank Leigh (*Norman Osgood*), Augustus Phillips (*Bob Manning*), Howard Davies (*Harrison Kirk*), Adele Farrington, Lillian Rich, Dorothy Hagan, Thomas Guise, Ralph McCullough, Edward Burns, Wilton Taylor. *Prod:* Pathé Exchange.

DICE OF DESTINY (1920). A crook's daughter, and her boy-friend, are persecuted by a police officer, who is a patient at the hospital where they both work, but they save his life and are pardoned. *With* H. B. Warner (*Jimmy Doyle*), Lillian Rich (*Nancy Preston*), Howard Davies (*Dave Monteith*), Harvey Clark (*Joe Caffey*), J. P. Lockney (*Bill Preston*), Claude Payton (*James Tierney*), Frederick Huntley, Rosemary Theby. *Prod:* Jesse Hampton Snr. for Pathé Exchange.

WHEN WE WERE TWENTY-ONE (1921). Comedy-drama of high life, involving an early case of "gold-digging." *Sc:* from the play by Henry V. Esmond. *Ph:* Victor Milner. *With* H. B. Warner (*Richard Carewe*), Claire Anderson (*Phyllis*), James Morrison (*Richard Audaine*), Christine Mayo (*Kara Glynesk*), Claude Payton (*Dave*), Minna Grey (*Mrs. Ericson*). *Prod:* Pathé Exchange. Re-made in 1930 as THE TRUTH ABOUT YOUTH (*Dir:* William A. Seiter).

THE MISTRESS OF SHENSTONE (1921). Romantic story, set in Cornwall, in which a titled woman comes to love the man who inadvertently caused her husband's death. *Sc:* from the novel by Florence L. Barclay. *Ph:* J. D. Jennings. *With* Pauline Frederick (*Lady Myra Ingleby*), Roy Stewart (*Jim Airth*), Emmett C. King (*Sir Deryck Brand*), Arthur Clayton (*Ronald Ingram*), John Willink (*Billy Cathcart*), Helen Wright (*Margaret O'Mara*), Rosa Gore, Helen Muir, Lydia Yeamans Titus. *Prod:* Robertson-Cole Co. 6r.

SALVAGE (1921). Melodrama involving adoption, assumed identity, love and sacrifice. *Sc:* Daniel F. Whitcomb. *Ph:* J. D. Jennings. *With* Pauline Frederick (*Bernice Ridgeway/Kate Martin*), Ralph Lewis (*Cyrus Ridgeway*), Milton Sills (*Fred Martin*), Helen Stone (*Ruth Martin*), Rose Cade (*Tessie*), Raymond Hatton (*The Cripple*), Hobart Kelly (*The Baby*). *Prod:* Robertson-Cole Co. 6r.

THE STING OF THE LASH (1921). Mining and marital drama. Wife's struggle to keep her weak husband up to scratch includes giving him the whipping of the title. *Sc:* H. Tipton Steck (story by Harvey Gates). *Ph:* Dev Jennings. *With* Pauline Frederick (*Dorothy Keith*), Clyde Fillmore (*Joel Gant*), Lawson Butt (*Rhodes*), Lionel Belmore (*Ben Ames*), Jack Richardson (*Seeley*), Edwin Stevens (*Daniel Keith*), Betty Hall (*Crissy, age six*), Evelyn McCoy (*Crissy, age ten*), Percy Challenger (*Rorke*). *Prod:* Robertson-Cole Co. 6r.

TOL'ABLE DAVID (1921). Rural drama of Virginia mountain life, climaxed by a "mail must get through" pursuit and fight, proving the manhood of young David. *Sc:* Edmund Goulding, Henry King, and—on previous draft—D. W. Griffith (story by Joseph Hergesheimer). *Ph:* Henry Cronjager. *Ed:* Duncan Mansfield. *With* Richard Barthelmess (*David Kinemon*), Gladys Hulette (*Esther Hatburn*), Walter P. Lewis (*Iscah Hatburn*), Ernest Torrence (*Luke Hatburn*), Ralph Yearsley (*Luke's brother*), Forrest Robinson (*Grandpa Hatburn*), Laurence Eddinger (*Senator Gault*), Edmund Gurney (*David's father*), Warner Richmond (*David's brother*), Marion Abbott (*David's mother*), Lassie (*The Dog*). *Prod:* Henry King for Inspiration Pictures (First National release). 7r. Re-made in 1930 (*Dir:* John G. Blystone). Possibly, Hal Roach comedy TOL'ABLE ROMEO (1926) refers.

THE SEVENTH DAY (1922). Romantic quadrangle society drama, with New England sea-coast setting. *Sc:* Edmund Goulding (story by Porter Emerson Browne). *Ph:* Henry Cronjager. *Ed:* Duncan Mansfield. *With* Richard Barthelmess (*John Alden Jr.*), Frank Losee (*Uncle Jim Alden*), Leslie Stowe (*Uncle Ned*), Tammany Young (*Donald Peabody*), George Stewart (*Reggie Van Zandt*), Alfred Schmid (*Monty Pell*), Anne Cornwall (*Betty Alden*), Louise Huff (*Patricia Vane*), Grace Barton, Patterson Dial, Teddie Gerard. *Prod:* Henry King for Inspiration Pictures (First National release). 6r.

SONNY (1922). Dual look-alike role for Barthelmess; one of him takes his dead friend's place in the household. *Sc:* Frances Marion, Henry King (play by George V. Hobart). *Ph:* Henry Cronjager. *Art dir:* Charles Osborne Seessel. *Ed:* Duncan Mansfield. *With* Richard Barthelmess (*Sonny (Charles Crosby)/ Joe*), Margaret Seddon (*Mrs. Crosby*), Pauline Garon (*Florence Crosby*), Lucy Fox (*Madge Craig*), Herbert Grimwood (*Harper Craig*), Patterson Dial (*Alicia*), Fred Nicholls (*Summers*), James Terbell, Margaret Elizabeth Falconer, Virginia Magee. *Prod:* Henry King for Inspiration Pictures (First National release). 7r.

THE BOND BOY (1922). Melodrama of poverty, murder and wrongful conviction; also a happy ending. *Sc:* Charles E. Whittaker (story by George Washington Ogden). *Ph:* Roy Overbaugh. *Art dir:* Charles Osborne Seessel. *Ed:* Duncan Mansfield. *With* Richard Barthelmess (*Peter Newbolt/Joe Newbolt, his son*), Charles Hill Mailes (*Isom Chase*),

Ned Sparks (*Cyrus Morgan*), Lawrence D'Orsay (*Colonel Price*), Robert Williamson (*Lawyer Hammer*), Leslie King (*District Attorney*), Jerry Sinclair (*Sheriff*), Thomas Maguire, Lucia Backus Seger, Virginia Magee, Mary Alden, Mary Thurman. *Prod:* Henry King for Inspiration Pictures (First National release). 7r.

FURY (1922). Sea adventure and a personality struggle between tough father and sensitive son. *Sc:* Edmund Goulding. *Ph:* Roy Overbaugh. *Art dir:* Robert M. Haas. *Ed:* Duncan Mansfield. *With* Richard Barthelmess (*Boy Leyton*), Tyrone Power Sr. (*Captain Leyton*), Pat Hartigan (*Morgan*), Barry Macollum (*Looney Luke*), Dorothy Gish (*Minnie*), Jessie Arnold (*Boy's Mother*), Harry Blakemore (*Mr. Hop*), Adolph Milar, Ivan Linow, Emily Fitzroy, Lucia Backus Seger, Patterson Dial. *Prod:* Henry King for Inspiration Pictures (First National release). 9r.

THE WHITE SISTER (1923). Romantic drama, shot on Italian locations. *Sc:* George V. Hobart, Charles E. Whittaker (novel by Francis Marion Crawford). *Ph:* Roy Overbaugh. *Art dir:* Robert M. Haas. *Ed:* Duncan Mansfield. *With* Lillian Gish (*Angela Chiaromonte*), Ronald Colman (*Capt. Giovanni Severini*), Gail Kane (*Marchesa di Mola*), J. Barney Sherry (*Monsignor Saracinesca*), Charles Lane (*Prince Chiaromonte*), Juliette La Violette (*Madame Bernard*), Signor Serena (*Prof. Ugo Severini*), Alfredo Bertone, Ramon Ibanez, Alfredo Martinelli, Carloni Talli, Giovanni Viccola, Antonio Barda, Giacomo D'Attino, Michele Gualdi, Giuseppe Pavoni, Francesco Socinus, Sheik Mahomet, James

Abbe, Duncan Mansfield. *Prod:* Henry King for Inspiration Pictures (Metro release). 13r (roadshow). 10r (release). Previous version 1915 (*Prod:* Essanay). Re-made 1933 (*Dir:* Victor Fleming).

ROMOLA (1924). Historical romance of Italy in the days of Savonarola; made in Italy also. *Sc:* Will M. Ritchey (novel written in 1862 by George Eliot). *Art dir:* Robert M. Haas. *With* Lillian Gish (*Romola*), Dorothy Gish (*Tessa*), William H. Powell (*Tito Melema*), Ronald Colman (*Carlo Buccellini*), Charles Lane (*Baldassarre Calvo*), Herbert Grimwood (*Savonarola*), Bonaventure Ibanez (*Bardo Bardi*), Frank Puglia, Amelia Summerville, Angelo Scatigna, Edulilo Mucci, Tina Rinaldi, Alfredo Bertone, Alfredo Martinelli, Ugo Uccellini. *Prod:* Henry King for Inspiration Pictures (Metro-Goldwyn release). 12r.

SACKCLOTH AND SCARLET (1925). The eternal triangle in a rural setting (Paradise Valley). *Sc:* Tom Geraghty, Jules Furthman, Julie Herne (novel by George Gibbs). *Ph:* Robert Kurrle, William Schurr. *Art dir:* Robert M. Haas. *With* Alice Terry (*Joan Freeman*), Orville Caldwell (*Stephen Edwards*), Dorothy Sebastian (*Polly Freeman*), Otto Matiesen (*Etienne Fochard*), Kathleen Kirkham (*Beatrice Selignac*), John Miljan (*Samuel Curtis*), Clarissa Selwynne (*Miss Curtis*), Jack Huff (*Jack*). *Prod:* Henry King (for Robert Kane, Paramount). 7r.

ANY WOMAN (1925). A girl is chased by "wolves" but finds true love with the inventor of a soft drink called "Here's How." *Sc:* Jules Furthman, Beatrice Van (story by Arthur Somers Roche). *Ph:* Ernest Haller, William Schurr. *With* Alice Terry (*Ellen Linden*), Ernest Gillen (*Tom Galloway*), Margarita Fisher (*Mrs. Rand*), Lawson Butt (*James Rand*), Aggie Herring (*Mrs. Galloway*), James Neill (*William Linden*), De Sacia Mooers (*Mrs. Phillips*), Henry Kolker, Thelma Morgan, George Periolat, Lucille Hutton, Arthur Hoyt, Malcolm Denny. *Prod:* Henry King (for Robert Kane, Paramount). 6r.

STELLA DALLAS (1925). Six-handkerchief classic of mother-love. *Sc:* Frances Marion (novel by Olive Higgins Prouty). *Ph:* Arthur Edeson. *Ed:* Stuart Heisler. *With* Ronald Colman (*Stephen Dallas*), Belle Bennett (*Stella Dallas*), Alice Joyce (*Helen Morrison*), Jean Hersholt (*Ed Munn*), Beatrix Pryor (*Mrs. Grosvenor*), Lois Moran (*Laurel Dallas*), Douglas Fairbanks Jr. (*Richard Grosvenor*), Vera Lewis, Maurice Murphy, Jack Murphy, Newton Hall, Charles Hatten, Robert Gillette, Winston Miller. *Prod:* Samuel Goldwyn (United Artists release). 11r. Re-made by Goldwyn 1937 (*Dir:* King Vidor). Also long-running radio soap opera.

PARTNERS AGAIN, WITH POTASH AND PERLMUTTER (1926). Once-popular farce-comedy team—in this episode of a Goldwyn series, partners in the automobile business. *Sc:* Frances Marion (play, "Partners Again," by Montague Glass and Jules Eckert Goodman). *Ph:* Arthur Edeson. *With* George Sidney (*Abe Potash*), Alexander Carr (*Mawruss Perlmutter*), Betty Jewel (*Hattie Potash*), Allan Forrest (*Dan*), Robert Schable (*Schenckmann*), Lillian Elliott (*Rosie Potash*), Earl Metcalf (*Aviator*), Lew Brice, Gilbert Clayton, Anna Gilbert. *Prod:* Samuel Goldwyn

(United Artists release). 6r.

THE WINNING OF BARBARA
WORTH (1926). Western drama with
a love story set against an adventure of
unscrupulous speculation in desert ir-
rigation. *Sc:* Frances Marion (story by
Harold Bell Wright). *Ph:* George Barnes.
Art dir: Karl Oscar Borg. *With* Ronald
Colman (*William Holmes*), Vilma Banky
(*Barbara Worth*), Charles Lane (*Jef-
ferson Worth*), Paul McAllister (*The
Seer*), E. J. Ratcliffe (*James Green-
field*), Gary Cooper (*Abe Lee*), Clyde
Cook, Erwin Connelly, Sam Blum, Ed-
win Brody. *Prod:* Samuel Goldwyn
(United Artists release). 9r.

THE MAGIC FLAME (1927). Colourful romantic tale of circus life and
Royal intrigues, with Banky pursued
by one man (a prince) but in love
with another (a clown); both are played
by Colman, long before his double role
in *The Prisoner of Zenda. Sc:* June
Mathis, Bess Meredyth ("King Harle-
quin" by Rudolph Lothar). *Ph:* George
Barnes. *Art dir:* Carl Oscar Borg. *With*
Ronald Colman (*The Clown (Tito)/The
Count*), Vilma Banky (*The Aerial Artist,
Bianca*), Augustino Borgato (*The Ring-
master*), Gustav von Seyffertitz (*The
Chancellor*), Harvey Clarke (*The Aide*),
Shirley Palmer (*The Wife*), Cosmo Kyrle
Bellew (*The Husband*), George Davis,
Andre Cheron, Vadim Uraneff. *Prod:*
Samuel Goldwyn (United Artists re-
lease). 9r.

THE WOMAN DISPUTED (1928).
Period drama in which the heroine
sacrifices herself for Austria and her
true love. *Co-dir:* Sam Taylor. *Sc:* C.
Gardner Sullivan (play by Dennison
Clift, deriving in part from story "Boule

de suif" by Guy de Maupassant). *Ph:*
Oliver Marsh. *Art dir:* William Cameron
Menzies. *Ed:* Hal Kern. *Music:* Hugo
Riesenfeld. *With* Norma Talmadge
(*Mary Ann Wagner*), Gilbert Roland
(*Paul Hartman*), Arnold Kent (*Nika
Turgenov*), Boris De Fas (*The Passer-
by*), Michael Vavitch (*Father Roche*),
Gustav von Seyffertitz (*Otto Krueger*),
Gladys Brockwell (*The Countess*),
Nicholas Soussanin (*The Count*). *Prod:*
Henry King for Joseph M. Schenck
(United Artists). 9r. Released silent and
in version with music and sound effects.
Contemporary references say Taylor re-
shot last scenes only.

SHE GOES TO WAR (1929). War
drama about a society girl who replaces
one (drunken) lover, in his uniform
at the front, and finds a worthier partner there. *Sc:* Howard Estabrook, with
dialogue and titles by John Monk Saun-
ders (story by Rupert Hughes). *Ph:*
John Fulton, Tony Gaudio. *Art dir:*
Al D'Agostino, Robert M. Haas. *Ed:*
Lloyd Nosler. *With* Eleanor Boardman
(*Joan*), John Holland (*Tom Pike*),
Edmund Burns (*Reggie*), Alma Rubens
(*Rosie*), Al St. John (*Bill*), Glen Walters (*Katie*), Margaret Seddon (*Tom's
mother*), Yola D'Avril, Evelyn Hall,
Augustino Borgato, Dina Smirnova,
Yvonne Starke. *Prod:* Victor Halperin
and Edward Halperin for Inspiration
Pictures (United Artists release). 10r
(part-talking version), 9r (silent ver-
sion).

HELL HARBOR (1930). Romantic
melodrama, shot on location in Florida,
concerning a descendant of Morgan the
pirate and his headstrong daughter.
King's first full talkie. *Sc:* Clarke Sil-

vernail, Fred De Gresac, N. Brewster Morse (story, "Out of the Night" by Rida Johnson Young). *Ph:* John Fulton. *Art dir:* Robert M. Haas. *Ed:* Lloyd Nosler. *With* Lupe Velez (*Anita*), Jean Hersholt (*Joseph Horngold*), John Holland (*Bob Wade*), Gibson Gowland (*Harry Morgan*), Al St. John (*Bunion*), Harry Allen (*Peg-Leg*), Paul E. Burns (*Blinkey*), George Book-Asta, Rondo Hatton, Habanera Sextette. *Prod:* Inspiration Pictures (United Artists release). 92m.

THE EYES OF THE WORLD (1930). Ripe "sins of the fathers" melodrama, involving seduction, disfiguring and reconciliation. *Sc:* N. Brewster Morse, Clarke Silvernail (story by Harold Bell Wright). *Ph:* Ray June, John Fulton. *Ed:* Lloyd Nosler. *With* (Prologue): Eulalie Jenson (*Mrs. Rutledge*), Hugh Huntley (*James Rutledge*), Myra Hubert (*Myra*), Florence Roberts (*Maid*). (Story): Una Merkel (*Sybil*), Nance O'Neil (*Myra*), John Holland (*Aaron King*), Fern Andra (*Mrs. Taine*), Hugh Huntley (*James Rutledge*), Frederic Burt, Brandon Hurst, William Jeffrey. *Prod:* Sol Lesser for Inspiration Pictures (United Artists release). 80m.

LIGHTNIN' (1930). Sentimental comedy-drama of a drunkard's difficulties with his wife and work; all happily reconciled in the last reel. King's first for the Fox Film Corporation. *Sc:* S. N. Behrman, Sonya Levien (play by Winchell Smith and Frank Bacon). *Ph:* Chester Lyons. *Art dir:* Harry Oliver. *Ed:* Louis Loeffler. *With* Will Rogers ("*Lightnin'* " *Bill Jones*), Louise Dresser (*Mrs. Jones*), Joel McCrea (*John Marvin*), Helen Cohan (*Milly Jones*),

Jason Robards Sr. (*Thomas*), Luke Cosgrave (*Zeb*), J. M. Kerrigan (*Lem Townsend*), Ruth Warren, Sharon Lynn, Joyce Compton, Rex Bell, Frank Campeau, Goodee Montgomery, Philip Tead, Walter Percival, Charlotte Walker, Blanche Le Clair, Bruce Warren, Antica Nast, Moon Carroll, Bess Flowers, Gwendolyn Faye, Roxanne Curtis. *Prod:* Fox. 94m. Silent version 1925 (*dir:* John Ford).

MERELY MARY ANN (1931). Sentimental, wistful romance of an orphan "slavey" and a hopeful but penniless composer. *Sc:* Jules Furthman (play by Israel Zangwill). *Ph:* John F. Seitz. *Ed:* Frank Hull. *With* Janet Gaynor (*Mary Ann*), Charles Farrell (*John Lonsdale*), Beryl Mercer (*Mrs. Leadbatter*), J. M. Kerrigan, Lorna Balfour, Arnold Lucy, Tom Whitely, G. P. Huntley Jr., Harry Rosenthal. *Prod:* Fox. 75m. Silent versions 1916 (*dir:* John G. Adolfi) and 1920 (*dir:* Edward J. LeSaint).

OVER THE HILL (1931). A modernised conception of "Over the Hill to the Poorhouse," with mother-love overcoming all. *Sc:* Tom Barry, Jules Furthman (poem by Will Carleton). *Ph:* John F. Seitz. *Ed:* Frank Hull. *With* Mae Marsh (*Ma Shelby*), James Kirkwood (*Pa Shelby*), James Dunn (*Johnny Shelby*), Sally Eilers (*Isabel Potter*), Edward Crandall, Claire Maynard, Olin Howland, Joan Peers, Joe Hachey, Tom Conlon, Julius Molnar, Marilyn Harris, Nancy Irish, Eula Guy, William Pawley, George Reed, Douglas Walton, David Hartford. *Prod:* Fox. 89m. Silent version 1920 (*dir:* Harry Millarde).

THE WOMAN IN ROOM 13 (1932). Murder mystery with husband taking blame for wife's apparent guilt. *Sc:* Guy Bolton (play by Samuel Shipman, Max Marcin, Percival Wilde). *Ph:* John F. Seitz. *Ed:* Al de Gateno. *With* Elissa Landi (*Laura*), Ralph Bellamy (*John Bruce*), Neil Hamilton (*Paul Ramsey*), Myrna Loy (*Sari Lodar*), Gilbert Roland (*Victor Legrand*), Walter Walker, Luis Alberni, Charley Grapewin. *Prod:* Fox. 67m. Silent version 1920 (*dir:* Frank Lloyd).

STATE FAIR (1933). First, non-musical, version of perennial tale of one family's romances, disappointments and minor triumphs during State Fair week. *Sc:* Paul Green & Sonya Levien (novel by Phil Stong). *Ph:* Hal Mohr. *Art dir:* Duncan Cramer. *Ed:* R. W. Bischoff. *Music:* Ray Flynn. *With* Will Rogers (*Abel Frake*), Janet Gaynor (*Margy Frake*), Lew Ayres (*Pat Gilbert*), Sally Eilers (*Emily Joyce*), Norman Foster (*Wayne Frake*), Louise Dresser (*Melissa Frake*), Frank Craven, Victor Jory, Frank Melton, John Sheehan, Erville Anderson, Harry Holman, Hobart Cavanaugh. *Prod:* Winfield Sheehan for Fox. 80m. Musical versions 1945 (*dir:* Walter Lang) and 1962 (*dir:* Jose Ferrer).

I LOVED YOU WEDNESDAY (1933). Romantic quadrangle comedy-drama set in Paris, New York and South America. *Co-dir:* William Cameron Menzies. *Sc:* Philip Klein, Horace Jackson (play by Molly Ricardel and William Du Bois). *Ph:* Hal Mohr. *Ed:* Frank Hull. *With* Warner Baxter (*Philip Fletcher*), Elissa Landi (*Vicki Meredith*), Victor Jory (*Randall Williams*), Miriam Jordan (*Cynthia Williams*), Laura Hope Crews (*Doc Mary Hanson*). *Prod:* Fox. 80m.

(Production designer Menzies received special billing on several films at this period.)

CAROLINA (1934). Comedy-romance of a proud but impoverished Southern family. *Sc:* Reginald Berkeley (play, "The House of Connelly" by Paul Green). *Ph:* Hal Mohr. *Ed:* Robert Bassler. *Music:* Louis de Francesco. *With* Janet Gaynor (*Joanna Tate*), Lionel Barrymore (*Bob Connelly*), Robert Young (*Will Connelly*), Richard Cromwell (*Allen*), Henrietta Crosman (*Mrs. Connelly*), Mona Barrie (*Virginia*), Stepin Fetchit (*Scipio*), Russell Simpson, Ronnie and Jackie Cosbey, Shirley Temple, Almeda Fowler, Alden Chase. *Prod:* Fox. 85m.

MARIE GALANTE (1934). An innocent girl is caught up in espionage and sabotage; Ketti Gallian's bid for stardom was less successful than other players debuting under King's direction. *Sc:* Reginald Berkeley (novel by Jacques Deval). *Ph:* John F. Seitz. *Music:* Arthur Lange. *With* Spencer Tracy (*Crawbett*), Ketti Gallian (*Marie Galante*), Ned Sparks (*Plosser*), Helen Morgan (*Tapia*), Sig Rumann, Leslie Fenton, Arthur Byron, Robert Lorraine, Jay C. Flippen, Frank Darien, Stepin Fetchit, Tito Coral. *Prod:* Winfield Sheehan for Fox. 88m.

ONE MORE SPRING (1935). Wry depression-era comedy concerns an odd trio living in a tool-shed in New York City's Central Park. *Sc:* Edwin Burke (novel by Robert Nathan). *Ph:* John F. Seitz. *Music:* Arthur Lange. *With* Janet Gaynor (*Elizabeth*), Warner Baxter (*Otkar*), Walter Woolf King (*Rosenberg*), Jane Darwell (*Mrs. Sweeney*),

Roger Imhof (*Mr. Sweeney*), Grant Mitchell, Rosemary Ames, John Qualen, Nick Foran, Astrid Allwyn, Stepin Fetchit, Jayne Regan, Lee Kohlmar. *Prod:* Winfield Sheehan for Fox. 87m.

WAY DOWN EAST (1935). Once again, the illegitimate baby, the despised heroine and the climactic rescue from the ice floes. *Sc:* Howard Estabrook, William Hurlbut (play by Lottie Blair Parker). *Ph:* Ernest Palmer. *Art dir:* William Darling. *Ed:* Robert Bischoff. *Music:* Oscar Bradley. *With* Rochelle Hudson (*Anna Moore*), Henry Fonda (*David Bartlett*), Slim Summerville (*Constable Seth Holcomb*), Edward Trevor (*Lennox Sanderson*), Margaret Hamilton (*Martha Perkins*), Russell Simpson (*Squire Bartlett*), Andy Devine, Spring Byington, Astrid Allwyn, Sara Haden, William Benedict, Al Lydell, Harry C. Bradley, Phil La Toska, Clem Bevans, Vera Lewis, Seymour and Corncob. *Prod:* Winfield Sheehan for Fox. 80m. Silent version 1920 (*dir:* D. W. Griffith).

THE COUNTRY DOCTOR (1936). The daily life of a doctor and his community in Northern Canada. *Sc:* Sonya Levien (story idea by Charles E. Blake). *Ph:* John F. Seitz, Daniel B. Clarke. *Ed:* Barbara McLean. *Music:* Louis Silvers. Dionne Quintuplets photographed under the technical supervision of Dr. Allan Roy Dafoe. *With* Jean Hersholt (*Dr. John Luke*), Dorothy Peterson (*Nurse Kennedy*), June Lang (*Mary*), Michael Whalen (*Tony*), Slim Summerville (*Ogden*), John Qualen (*Asa Wyatt*), Montagu Love (*Sir Basil*), Robert Barrat, Jane Darwell, Joseph Sawyer, Kane Richmond, J. Anthony Hughes, George

Chandler, Frank Reicher, David Torrence, Helen Jerome Eddy, Aileen Carlyle, George Meeker, William Benedict, Dionne Quintuplets. *Prod:* Darryl F. Zanuck, Nunnally Johnson for 20th Century-Fox. 110m.

RAMONA (1936). Long-lived romance of Indian life became King's (and his studio's) first Technicolor film. *Sc:* Lamar Trotti (novel by Helen Hunt Jackson). *Ph:* Chester Lyons, William V. Skall. *Art dir:* Duncan Cramer. *Ed:* Alfred de Gateno. *Music:* Alfred Newman. *With* Loretta Young (*Ramona*), Don Ameche (*Alessandro*), Kent Taylor (*Felipe Moreno*), Pauline Frederick (*Senora Moreno*), Jane Darwell, Katherine De Mille, Victor Kilian, John Carradine, J. Carroll Naish, Russell Simpson, Chief Thunder Cloud, Charles Waldron, Pedro de Cordoba, Claire Du Brey, William Benedict, Robert Spindola. *Prod:* Sol M. Wurtzel for 20th Century-Fox. 90m. Technicolor. Silent versions 1910 (*dir:* D. W. Griffith), 1916 (*dir:* Donald Crisp), and 1928 (An Inspiration Picture, *dir:* Edwin Carewe).

LLOYDS OF LONDON (1936). Heavily fictionalised history of Georgian England, with the fledgling insurance company doing its bit before Trafalgar. *Sc:* Ernest Pascal, Walter Ferris (story by Curtis Kenyon). *Ph:* Bert Glennon. *Art dir:* William Darling. *Sets:* Thomas Little. *Ed:* Barbara McLean. *Music:* Louis Silvers. *With* Tyrone Power (*Jonathan Blake*), Madeleine Carroll (*Lady Elizabeth*), Freddie Bartholomew (*Jonathan as a boy*), Sir Guy Standing (*Angerstein*), C. Aubrey Smith (*Queensberry*), Virginia Field (*Polly*), George

Sanders (*Lord Everett Stacy*), Douglas Scott (*Nelson*), J. M. Kerrigan, Una O'Connor, E. E. Clive, Miles Mander, Montagu Love, Lumsden Hare, Gavin Muir, Will Stanton, John Burton, Murray Kinnell, Ralph Cooper, Fay Chaldecott, Yorke Sherwood, May Beatty, Reginald Barlow, Billy Bevan, Robert Greig, Hugh Huntley, Elsa Buchanan, Arthur Hohl, Charles Crocker, Holmes Herbert, Georges Renavent, Lester Matthews, Forrester Harvey. *Prod:* Darryl F. Zanuck and Kenneth MacGowan for 20th Century-Fox. 115m.

SEVENTH HEAVEN (1937). The love of a waif and a street-cleaner under the stars of Paris. *Sc:* Melville Baker (play by Austin Strong). *Ph:* Merritt Gerstad. *Art dir:* William Darling. *Ed:* Barbara McLean. *Music:* Louis Silvers. *With* Simone Simon (*Diane*), James Stewart (*Chico*), Gale Sondergaard (*Nana*), Jean Hersholt (*Father Chevillon*), Gregory Ratoff (*Boul*), John Qualen ("*Sewer Rat*"), J. Edward Bromberg, Victor Kilian, Sig Rumann, Mady Christians, Thomas Beck, Rafaela Ottiano, Rollo Lloyd, Georges Renavent, Edward Keane, Irving Bacon, John Hamilton, Paul Porcasi, Will Stanton, Leonid Snegoff, Adrienne D'Ambricourt. *Prod:* Darryl F. Zanuck, Raymond Griffith for 20th Century-Fox. 102m. Silent version 1927 (*dir:* Frank Borzage).

IN OLD CHICAGO (1938). Quasi-historial spectacle, climaxed by the fire begun when Mrs. O'Leary's cow kicked a lamp. *Sc:* Lamar Trotti, Sonya Levien. *Ph:* J. Peverell Marley. *Art dir:* William Darling, Rudolph Sternad. *Ed:* Barbara McLean. *Music:* Louis Silvers (with songs by Mack Gordon & Harry Revel,

Sidney Mitchell & Lew Pollack). *With* Tyrone Power (*Dion O'Leary*), Alice Faye (*Belle Fawcett*), Don Ameche (*Jack O'Leary*), Alice Brady (*Molly O'Leary*), Andy Devine (*Pickle Bixby*), Brian Donlevy (*Gil Warren*), Phyllis Brooks (*Ann Colby*), Tom Brown, Sidney Blackmer, J. Anthony Hughes, Berton Churchill, Spencer Charters, June Storey, Paul Hurst, Tyler Brooke, Bobs Watson, Billy Watson, Gene Reynolds, Madame Sultewan, Rondo Hatton, Thelma Manning, Ruth Gillette, Charles Hummel Wilson, Eddie Collins, Scott Mattraw, Joe Twerp, Charles Lane, Frank Dae, Harry Stubbs, Francis Ford, Joe King, Robert Murphy, Wade Boteler, Gustav von Seyffertitz, Russell Hicks. *Prod:* Darryl F. Zanuck, Kenneth MacGowan for 20th Century-Fox. 115m.

ALEXANDER'S RAGTIME BAND (1938). The trials and triumphs of a mythical dance band, with lots of Irving Berlin music. *Sc:* Kathryn Scola, Lamar Trotti, Richard Sherman. *Ph:* J. Peverell Marley. *Art dir:* Bernard Herzbrun, Boris Leven. *Ed:* Barbara McLean. *Music:* Alfred Newman (songs with music and lyrics by Irving Berlin). *With* Tyrone Power (*Alexander-Roger Grant*), Alice Faye (*Stella Kirby*), Don Ameche (*Charlie Dwyer*), Ethel Merman (*Jerry Allen*), Jack Haley (*Davey Lane*), Jean Hersholt (*Prof. Heinrich*), Helen Westley, John Carradine, Paul Hurst, Wally Vernon, Ruth Terry, Douglas Fowley, Chick Chandler, Eddie Collins, Joseph Crehan, Robert Gleckler, Dixie Dunbar, Joe King, Grady Sutton, Donald Douglas, Charles Coleman, Stanley Andrews, Charles Williams, Jane Jones, Otto Fries, Mel Kalish, Selmar Jackson, Tyler

Randolph Scott in
JESSE JAMES

Brooke. *Prod:* Darryl F. Zanuck, Harry Joe Brown for 20th Century-Fox. 105m. JESSE JAMES (1939). Story of the outlaw James brothers, semi-factually based on considerable research. *Sc:* Nunnally Johnson (historical data assembled by Rosalind Shaffer & Jo Frances James). *Ph:* W. Howard Greene, George Barnes. *Art dir:* William Darling, George Dudley. *Ed:* Barbara McLean. *Music:* Louis Silvers. *With* Tyrone Power (*Jesse James*), Henry Fonda (*Frank James*), Nancy Kelly (*Zee*), Randolph Scott (*Will Wright*), Henry Hull (*Major Cobb*), Brian Donlevy (*Barshee*), John Carradine (*Bob Ford*), Jane Darwell, Donald Meek, Slim Summerville, J. Edward Bromberg, Charles Middleton, George Breakston, Lon Chaney Jr., John Russell, George Chandler, Charles Tannen, Claire Du Brey, Willard Robertson,

Harold Goodwin, Spencer Charters, Ernest Whitman, Eddy Waller, Paul Burns, Arthur Aylesworth, Charles Halton, Harry Tyler, Virginia Brissac, Edward Le Saint, Erville Alderson, John Elliott. *Prod:* Darryl F. Zanuck, Nunnally Johnson for 20th Century-Fox. 105m. Technicolor. Re-made 1957 as THE TRUE STORY OF JESSE JAMES (G.B.: THE JAMES BROTHERS), (*dir:* Nicholas Ray).

STANLEY AND LIVINGSTONE (1939). Again semi-factual, with reporter Stanley seeking missing doctor Livingstone in Africa. *Sc:* Philip Dunne, Julien Josephson (research and outline by Hal Long, Sam Hellman). *Ph:* George Barnes. *Art dir:* William Darling, George Dudley. *Ed:* Barbara McLean. *Music:* Robert R. Bennett, David Buttolph, Louis Silvers. *With* Spencer Tracy (*Henry M. Stanley*), Nancy Kelly (*Eve Kingsley*), Richard Greene (*Gareth Tyce*), Walter Brennan (*Jeff Slocum*), Charles Coburn (*Lord Tyce*), Sir Cedric Hardwicke (*Dr. David Livingstone*), Henry Hull (*James G. Bennett Jr.*), Henry Travers, Miles Mander, David Torrence, Holmes Herbert, Montague Shaw, Brandon Hurst, Hassan Said, Paul Harvey, Paul Stanton, Russell Hicks, Frank Dae, Joseph Crehan, Robert Middlemass, Frank Jacquet, Clarence Derwent. *Prod:* Darryl F. Zanuck, Kenneth MacGowan for 20th Century-Fox. 101m. LITTLE OLD NEW YORK (1940). Very little fact in a romance of steamship days on the Hudson River with inventor Fulton shown as a surprisingly young man. *Sc:* Harry Tugend (play by Rida Johnson Young, adaptation by John L. Balderston). *Ph:* Leon Shamroy. *Art dir:* Richard Day. *Ed:* Barbara McLean. *Music:* Alfred Newman. *With* Alice Faye (*Pat O'Day*), Fred MacMurray (*Charles Browne*), Richard Greene (*Robert Fulton*), Brenda Joyce (*Harriet Livingston*), Andy Devine ("*Commodore*"), Henry Stephenson (*Robert R. Livingston*), Fritz Feld, Ward Bond, Clarence Hummel Wilson, Robert Middlemass, Roger Imhof, Theodore von Eltz, Arthur Aylesworth, Ben Carter, Stanley Andrews, O. G. Hendrian, Harry Tyler, Victor Kilian, Paul Sutton, Tyler Brooke, Jody Gilbert, Herbert Ashley, Virginia Brissac, Herbert Heywood. *Prod:* Darryl F. Zanuck for 20th Century-Fox. 100m. Previous version 1923 (*dir:* Sidney Olcott).

MARYLAND (1940). Simple horse raising and riding story, set in the magnificent countryside north of Baltimore. *Sc:* Ethel Hill, Jack Andrews. *Ph:* George Barnes, Ray Rennahan. *Art dir:* Richard Day, Wiard Ihnen. *Ed:* Barbara McLean. *Music:* Alfred Newman. *With* Walter Brennan (*William Stewart*), Fay Bainter (*Charlotte Danfield*), Brenda Joyce (*Linda*), John Payne (*Lee Danfield*), Charlie Ruggles (*Dick Piper*), Hattie McDaniel (*Hattie*), Marjorie Weaver, Sidney Blackmer, Ben Carter, Ernest Whitman, Paul Harvey, Robert Lowery, Spencer Charters, Ed Thorgerson, Frank Thomas, Stanley Andrews, Cliff Clark, Grace Hayle, William Davidson, Bobby Anderson, Clarence Muse, Dickie Jones, Patsy Barber, Erville Alderson, Zack Williams, Anita Brown, Darby Jones, Thaddeus Jones, Mildred Glover, E. E. Clive, Gladden James, George Reed, Helen Koford, Madame Sultewan, Arie Lee Branche,

Clinton Rosemond, Jesse Graves, Floyd Schachelford, Olive Ball, Charles Moore. *Prod:* Darryl F. Zanuck, Gene Markey for 20th Century-Fox. 92m. Technicolor.

CHAD HANNA (1940). Adventure-romance of circus life; conventional but strong on local colour. *Sc:* Nunnally Johnson (story "Red Wheels Rolling" by Walter D. Edmonds). *Ph:* Ernest Palmer, Ray Rennahan. *Art dir:* Richard Day. *Ed:* Barbara McLean. *Music:* David Buttolph. *With* Henry Fonda (*Chad Hanna*), Dorothy Lamour (*Albany Yates*), Linda Darnell (*Caroline*), Guy Kibbee (*Huguenine*), Jane Darwell (*Mrs. Huguenine*), John Carradine, Ted North, Roscoe Ates, Ben Carter, Frank Thomas, Olin Howland, Frank Conlan, Edward Conrad, Edward McWade, Ed Mundy, George Davis, Paul Burns, Sarah Padden, Leonard St. Leo, Elizabeth Abbott, Tully Marshall, Almira Sessions, Virginia Brissac, Si Jenks, Victor Kilian, Louis Mason, Charles Middleton, Harry Tyler, Eddy Waller, Alberta Gary. *Prod:* Darryl F. Zanuck, Nunnally Johnson for 20th Century-Fox. 86m. Technicolor.

A YANK IN THE R.A.F. (1941). Topical wartime romance actioner, an early case of the period's "hands across the sea." *Sc:* Darrell Ware, Karl Tunberg (story by Melville Crossman, pseudonym of Darryl F. Zanuck). *Ph:* Leon Shamroy. *Assoc. Ph:* Ronald Neame. *Art dir:* Richard Day, James Basevi. *Ed:* Barbara McLean. *Music:* (*and lyrics*) Leo Robin, Ralph Rainger. *With* Tyrone Power (*Tim Baker*), Betty Grable (*Carol Brown*), John Sutton (*Wing Commander Morley*), Reginald Gardiner (*Roger Phillby*), Donald Stuart (*Corporal Harry*

Baker), Richard Fraser (*Thorndyke*), Denis Green, Bruce Lester, Gilchrist Stuart, Lester Matthews, Ethel Griffies, Fortunio Bonanova, Ralph Byrd, Claude Allister, James Craven, Frederick Worlock, Morton Lowry, G. P. Huntley, Stuart Robertson, Dennis Hoey. *Prod:* Darryl F. Zanuck, Lou Edelman for 20th Century-Fox. 98m.

REMEMBER THE DAY (1941). Genuinely moving resume of a lady schoolteacher's life and love, with sentiment and humour finely balanced. *Sc:* Tess Slesinger, Frank Davis, Allan Scott (play by Philo Higley and Philip Dunning). *Ph:* George Barnes. *Art dir:* Richard Day. *Ed:* Barbara McLean. *Music:* Alfred Newman. *With* Claudette Colbert (*Nora Trinell*), John Payne (*Dan Hopkins*), John Shepperd (*Dewey Roberts*), Jane Seymour (*Mrs. Roberts*), Ann Todd (*Kate Hill*), Douglas Croft (*Dewey Roberts as a boy*), Anne Revere (*Miss Price*), Frieda Inescort, Harry Hayden, Francis Pierlot, Marie Blake, William Henderson, Chick Chandler, Selmar Jackson, William Halligan, George Ernest, Harry Tyler, Jody Gilbert, Irving Bacon, Paul Harvey, Thurston Hall, John Hiestand, Kay Linaker, Billy Dawson, George Chandler, Geraldine Wall. *Prod:* William Perlberg for 20th Century-Fox. 85m.

THE BLACK SWAN (1942). Rousing yarn of piracy on the high seas, just slightly tongue-in-cheek. *Sc:* Ben Hecht, Seton I. Miller (novel by Rafael Sabatini). *Ph:* Leon Shamroy. *Art dir:* Richard Day, James Basevi. *Ed:* Barbara McLean. *Music:* Alfred Newman. *With* Tyrone Power (*James Waring*), Maureen O'Hara (*Margaret Denby*), Laird Cregar

Tyrone Power and Maureen O'Hara seem unsure of George Sanders in THE BLACK SWAN

(*Capt. Henry Morgan*), Thomas Mitchell (*Tommy Blue*), George Sanders (*Capt. Billy Leech*), Anthony Quinn (*Wogan*), George Zucco (*Lord Denby*), Edward Ashley, Fortunio Bonanova, Stuart Robertson, Charles McNaughton, Frederick Worlock, Willie Fung, Charles Francis, Arthur Shields, Keith Hitchcock, John Burton, Cyril McLaglen, Clarence Muse, David Thursby, Olaf Hytten, Charles Irwin, Frank Leigh. *Prod:* Robert Bassler for 20th Century-Fox. 85m. Technicolor.

THE SONG OF BERNADETTE (1943). Story of the French peasant girl's vision of the Virgin Mary and its world-wide repercussions. *Sc:* George Seaton (novel by Franz Werfel). *Ph:* Arthur Miller. *Art dir:* James Basevi, William Darling. *Ed:* Barbara McLean. *Music:* Alfred Newman. *With* Jennifer Jones (*Bernadette*), William Eythe (*Antoine*), Charles Bickford (*Dean Peyramale*), Vincent Price (*Dutour*), Lee J. Cobb

(*Dr. Dozous*), Gladys Cooper (*Sister Vauzous*), Anne Revere (*Louise Soubirous*), Roman Bohnen (*François Soubirous*), Mary Anderson, Patricia Morison, Aubrey Mather, Charles Dingle, Edith Barrett, Sig Rumann, Blanche Yurka, Linda Darnell [uncredited], Ermadean Walters, Marcel Dalio, Pedro de Cordoba, Jerome Cowan, Charles Waldron, Moroni Olsen, Nana Bryant, Manart Kippen, Merrill Rodin, Nino Pipitone Jr., John Maxwell Hayes, Jean Del Val, Nestor Paiva, Tala Birell, Eula Morgan, Alan Napier, Dorothy Shearer, Frank Reicher, Charles La Torre, Nino Pipitone Sr., Edwin Stanley, Lionel Bramham, Ian Wolfe, Andre Charlot. *Prod:* William Perlberg for 20th Century-Fox. 156m.

WILSON (1944). Life of the U.S. President from Princeton days to great world events. *Sc:* Lamar Trotti. *Ph:* Leon Shamroy. *Art dir:* Wiard Ihnen, James Basevi. *Ed:* Barbara McLean. *Music:* Alfred Newman. *With* Alexander Knox (*Woodrow Wilson*), Charles Coburn (*Prof. Henry Holmes*), Geraldine Fitzgerald (*Edith Wilson*), Thomas Mitchell (*Joseph Tumulty*), Ruth Nelson (*Ellen Wilson*), Sir Cedric Hardwicke (*Sen. Henry Cabot Lodge*), Vincent Price (*William Gibbs McAdoo*), William Eythe (*George Felton*), Mary Anderson, Ruth Ford, Sidney Blackmer, Madeleine Forbes, Stanley Ridges, Eddie Foy Jr., Charles Halton, Thurston Hall, J. M. Kerrigan, James Rennie, Katherine Locke, Stanley Logan, Marcel Dalio, Edwin Maxwell, Clifford Brooke, Tonio Selwart, John Ince, Charles Miller, Francis X. Bushman, George Macready, Phyllis Brooks, Anne O'Neal, Arthur Loft, Russell Gage, Jameson Shade, Reginald Sheffield, Robert Middlemass, Matt Moore, George Anderson, Paul Everton, Robert Barron, Arthur Space, Roy Roberts, Frank Orth, Dewey Robinson, Cy Kendall, Emory Parnell, Ferris Taylor, Ken Christy, Guy D'Ennery, Antonio Filauri, Hilda Plowright, Joseph Greene, Gus Glassmire, Ralph Dunn, Isabel Randolph, Davidson Clark, Tony Hughes, Jess Lee Brooks, Gladden James, Frank Dawson, Larry McGrath, Ralph Linn, Josh Hardin, Russ Clark, Harold Schlickemeyer, Ed Mundy, Aubrey Mather, Jesse Graves, Del Henderson, John Ardell, George Matthews, John Whitney, William Forrest, Harry Tyler, Harry Carter, Jessie Grayson. *Prod:* Darryl F. Zanuck for 20th Century-Fox. 154m. Technicolor. (NOTE: After his return from war service, Zanuck is henceforth billed only on those pictures he personally produced.)

A BELL FOR ADANO (1945). Story of American army liberation of a small Italian town. *Sc:* Norman Reilly Raine, Lamar Trotti (novel by John Hersey). *Ph:* Joseph La Shelle. *Art dir:* Lyle R. Wheeler, Mark-Lee Kirk. *Ed:* Barbara McLean. *Music:* Alfred Newman. *With* John Hodiak (*Maj. Joppolo*), William Bendix (*Sgt. Borth*), Montague Banks (*Giuseppe*), Gene Tierney (*Tina*), Roman Bohnen (*Erba*), Fortunio Bonanova (*Gargano*), Hugo Haas, Henry Morgan, Richard Conte, Glenn Langan, Stanley Prager, Reed Hadley, Roy Roberts, Marcel Dalio, John Russell, Henry Armetta, Luis Alberni, Eduardo Ciannelli, Anne Demetrio, William Edmunds, Yvonne Vautrot, James Rennie, Charles La Torre, Charles Judels, Frank Jacquet,

Gino Corrado, Peter Cusanelli, Minor Watson, Grady Sutton, Joseph Milani, Edward Hyams. *Prod:* Louis D. Lighton, Lamar Trotti for 20th Century-Fox. 103m.

MARGIE (1946). Nostalgic musical look at the Twenties, in flashback from the Forties, as a mother recalls her youth to her daughter. *Sc:* F. Hugh Herbert (stories by Ruth McKenney and Richard Bransten). *Ph:* Charles G. Clarke. *Art dir:* James Basevi, J. Russell Spencer. *Ed:* Barbara McLean. *Music:* Alfred Newman. *With* Jeanne Crain (*Margie*), Glenn Langan (*Prof. Fontayne*), Lynn Bari (*Miss Palmer*), Alan Young (*Roy Hornsdale*), Barbara Lawrence (*Marybelle*), Conrad Janis (*Johnny*), Esther Dale (*Grandma McSweeney*), Hobart Cavanaugh, Ann Todd, Hattie McDaniel, Don Hayden, Hazel Dawn, Warren Mills, Richard Kelton, Vanessa Brown, Diana Herbert, Milton Parsons, Margaret Wells, Tom Stevenson, Cecil Weston. *Prod:* Walter Morosco for 20th Century-Fox. 94m. Technicolor.

CAPTAIN FROM CASTILE (1947). Rambling epic-scaled costume romance, partly shot on Mexican locations, with the book's violence and Inquisition brutality considerably toned down. *Sc:* Lamar Trotti (novel by Samuel Shellabarger). *Ph:* Charles G. Clarke, Arthur E. Arling. *Art dir:* Richard Day, James Basevi. *Ed:* Barbara McLean. *Music:* Alfred Newman. *With* Tyrone Power (*Pedro De Vargas*), Jean Peters (*Catana*), Cesar Romero (*Cortez*), Lee J. Cobb (*Juan Garcia*), John Sutton (*Diego De Silva*), Antonio Moreno (*Don Francisco*), Thomas Gomez (*Father Barto-*

lome), Alan Mowbray, Barbara Lawrence, George Zucco, Roy Roberts, Marc Lawrence, Robert Karnes, Fred Libby, John Laurenz, Virginia Brissac, Dolly Arriaga, John Burton, Jay Silverheels, Reed Hadley, Stella Inda, Mimi Aguglia. *Prod:* Lamar Trotti for 20th Century-Fox. 140m. Technicolor.

DEEP WATERS (1948). Mild romance, with romantic leads brought together by orphan boy, on the Maine coast (location shooting). *Sc:* Richard Murphy (novel "Spoonhandle" by Ruth Moore). *Ph:* Joseph La Shelle. *Art dir:* Lyle R. Wheeler, George W. Davis. *Ed:* Barbara McLean. *Music:* Cyril Mockridge. *With* Dana Andrews (*Hod Stilwell*), Jean Peters (*Ann Freeman*), Cesar Romero (*Joe Sanger*), Dean Stockwell (*Danny Mitchell*), Anne Revere (*Mary McKay*), Ed Begley (*Josh Hovey*), Leona Powers, Mae Marsh, Will Geer, Bruno Wick, Cliff Clark, Harry Tyler, Raymond Greenleaf. *Prod:* Samuel G. Engel for 20th Century-Fox. 85m.

PRINCE OF FOXES (1949). Fanciful fiction from fact, involving Cesare Borgia; King's return to Italian location filming after twenty-five years. *Sc:* Milton Krims (novel by Samuel Shellabarger). *Ph:* Leon Shamroy. *Art dir:* Lyle R. Wheeler, Mark-Lee Kirk. *Ed:* Barbara McLean. *Music:* Alfred Newman. *With* Tyrone Power (*Orsini*), Orson Welles (*Cesare Borgia*), Wanda Hendrix (*Camilla*), Felix Aylmer (*Varano*), Everett Sloane (*Belli*), Katina Paxinou (*Mona Zoppo*), Marina Berti (*Angela*), Leslie Bradley (*Esteban*), Rena Lennart, Njntsky, Giuseppe Faeti. *Prod:* Sol C. Siegel for 20th Century-Fox. 107m.

Italianate splendour: Felix Aylmer and Wanda Hendrix in PRINCE OF FOXES

TWELVE O'CLOCK HIGH (1949). Story of wartime bombing missions and the strain on the men involved. *Sc:* Sy Bartlett, Beirne Lay Jr. (from their novel). *Ph:* Leon Shamroy. *Art dir:* Lyle R. Wheeler, Maurice Ransford. *Ed:* Barbara McLean. *Music:* Alfred Newman. *With* Gregory Peck (*Gen. Savage*), Hugh Marlowe (*Lt. Col. Ben Gately*), Gary Merrill (*Col. Davenport*), Millard Mitchell (*Gen. Pritchard*), Dean Jagger (*Maj. Stovall*), Robert Arthur (*Sgt. McIllhenny*), Paul Stewart (*Capt. "Doc" Kaiser*), John Kellogg (*Maj. Cobb*), Robert Patton (*Lt. Bishop*), Lee Mac-Gregor, Sam Edwards, Roger Anderson, John Zilly, William Short, Richard Anderson, Lawrence Dobkin, Kenneth Tobey, Joyce MacKenzie, John McKee, Don Guadagno, Campbell Copelin, Peter Ortiz, Steve Clark, Don Hicks. *Prod:* Darryl F. Zanuck for 20th Century-Fox. 132m.

THE GUNFIGHTER (1950). Sombre, almost actionless western drama of Ringo, who would like to hang up his guns but is not allowed to. *Sc:* William Bowers, William Sellers (story by William Bowers and Andre De Toth). *Ph:* Arthur Miller. *Art dir:* Lyle R. Wheeler, Richard Irvine. *Ed:* Barbara McLean. *Music:* Alfred Newman. *With* Gregory Peck (*Jimmie Ringo*), Helen Westcott (*Peggy Walsh*), Millard Mitchell (*Sheriff Mark Strett*), Jean Parker (*Molly*), Mae Marsh (*Mrs. O'Brien*), Karl Malden (*Mac*), Skip Homeier (*Hunt Bromley*), Richard Jaeckel, Jean Inness, Verna Felton, Anthony Ross, Ellen Corby, Alan Hale Jr., David Clarke, John Pickard, B. G. Norman, Angela Clarke, Cliff Clark, Eddie Ehrhart, Alberto Morin,

Gregory Peck and Millard Mitchell in THE GUNFIGHTER

Ken Tobey, Michael Branden, Eddie Parkes, Ferris Taylor, Hank Patterson, Credda Zajac, Anne Whitfield, Kim Spaulding, Harry Shannon, Houseley Stevenson, James Millican, William Vedder, Ed Mundy. *Prod:* Nunnally Johnson for 20th Century-Fox. 84m.

I'D CLIMB THE HIGHEST MOUNTAIN (1951). Modulated Americana, with a light religious touch; shot on location in Georgia. *Sc:* Lamar Trotti (novel "Circuit Rider's Wife" by Corra Harris). *Ph:* Edward Cronjager. *Art dir:* Lyle R. Wheeler, Maurice Ransford. *Ed:* Barbara McLean. *Music:* Sol Kaplan. *With* Susan Hayward (*Mary Thompson*), William Lundigan (*William Asbury Thompson*), Rory Calhoun (*Jack Stark*), Barbara Bates (*Jenny Brock*), Gene Lockhart (*Mr. Brock*), Lynn Bari (*Mrs. Billywith*), Ruth Donnelly (*Glory White*), Kathleen Lockhart (*Mrs. Brock*), Alexander Knox (*Salter*), Jean Inness (*Mrs. Salter*), Frank Tweddell (*Dr. Fleming*), Jerry Vandiver, Richard Wilson, Kay and Fay Fogg, Dorothea Carolyn Sims, Thomas Syfan, Grady Starnes. *Prod:* Lamar Trotti for 20th Century-Fox. 88m. Technicolor.

DAVID AND BATHSHEBA (1951). Entry in Biblical cycle begun by De-Mille's *Samson and Delilah*; King David's adulterous love for Bathsheba causes trouble. *Sc:* Philip Dunne. *Ph:* Leon Shamroy. *Art dir:* Lyle R. Wheeler, George B. Davis. *Ed:* Barbara McLean. *Music:* Alfred Newman. *With* Gregory Peck (*David*), Susan Hayward (*Bathsheba*), Raymond Massey (*Nathan*), Kieron Moore (*Uriah*), James Robertson Justice (*Abishai*), Jayne Meadows (*Michal*), John Sutton (*Ira*), Dennis Hoey (*Joab*), Walter Talun (*Goliath*), Francis X. Bushman (*King Saul*), Gwen Verdon (*Dancer*), Paula Morgan, Teddy Infuhr, Gilbert Barnett, John Burton, Leo Pessin, Lumsden Hare, Paul Newlan, George Zucco, Allan Stone, Holmes Herbert, Harry Carter, Robert Stephenson, Richard Michelson, Dick Winters, John Duncan, James Craven. *Prod:* Darryl F. Zanuck for 20th Century-Fox. 116m. Technicolor.

WAIT TILL THE SUN SHINES, NELLIE (1952). Small-town saga with life revolving around the central figure, Wayne's kindly barber. *Sc:* Allan Scott, Maxwell Shane (novel "I Heard Them Sing" by Ferdinand Reyher). *Ph:* Leon Shamroy. *Art dir:* Lyle R. Wheeler, Maurice Ransford. *Ed:* Barbara McLean. *Music:* Alfred Newman. *With* David Wayne (*Ben Halper*), Jean Peters (*Nellie*), Hugh Marlowe (*Ed Jordan*), Albert Dekker (*Lloyd Slocum*), Helene Stanley (*Eadie Jordan*), Tommy Morton (*Benny Halper Jr.*), Joyce Mackenzie, Alan Hale Jr., Richard Karlan, Jim Maloney, Merry Anders, Warren Stevens, Charles Watts, David Wolfe, Dan White, Erik Nielsen, Jerrylyn Flannery, Noreen Corcoran, William Walker, James Griffith, Tommy Burr, Eugene Mazola, Maude Pickett, Mary Hain, Kermit Echols. *Prod:* George Jessel for 20th Century-Fox. 108m. Technicolor.

O. HENRY'S FULL HOUSE (G.B.: FULL HOUSE) (1952)—episode *The Gift of the Magi*, an ironic tale of a young couple's gifts to each other at Christmas. *Sc:* Walter Bullock (story by O. Henry). *Narrator:* John Steinbeck. *Ph:* Joseph MacDonald. *Art dir:* Lyle R. Wheeler. *Ed:* Barbara McLean. *Mu-*

sic: Alfred Newman. *With* Jeanne Crain (*Della*), Farley Granger (*Jim*), Fritz Feld, Sig Rumann, Harry Hayden. *Prod:* Andre Hakim for 20th Century-Fox. 117m.

THE SNOWS OF KILIMANJARO (1952). Hemingway story of a sick writer in Africa expanded to take in flashback chunks of "A Farewell to Arms." *Sc:* Casey Robinson (story by Ernest Hemingway). *Ph:* Leon Shamroy. *Art dir:* Lyle R. Wheeler, John De Cuir. *Ed:* Barbara McLean. *Music:* Bernard Herrmann. *With* Gregory Peck (*Harry*), Susan Hayward (*Helen*), Ava Gardner (*Cynthia*), Hildegarde Neff (*Countess Liz*), Leo G. Carroll (*Uncle Bill*), Torin Thatcher (*Johnson*), Ava Norring, Helene Stanley, Marcel Dalio, Vincente Gomez, Richard Allan, Leonard Carey, Paul Thompson, Emmett Smith, Victor Wood, Bert Freed, Maya Van Horn, Agnes Laury, Monique Chantal, Janine Grandel, John Dodsworth, Charles Bates, Lisa Ferraday, Ivan Lebedeff. *Prod:* Darryl F. Zanuck for 20th Century-Fox. 114m. Technicolor.

KING OF THE KHYBER RIFLES (1953). Adventure melodrama of half-caste officer in good old British India. *Sc:* Ivan Goff, Ben Roberts (novel by Talbot Mundy). *Ph:* Leon Shamroy. *Art dir:* Lyle R. Wheeler, Maurice Ransford. *Ed:* Barbara McLean. *Music:* Bernard Herrmann. *With* Tyrone Power (*Capt. King*), Terry Moore (*Susan Maitland*), Michael Rennie (*Gen. Maitland*), Guy Rolfe (*Kurram Khan*), John Justin (*Lt. Heath*), Richard Stapley, Murray Matheson, Frank De Kova, Argentina Brunetti, Sujata, Frank Lackteen, Gilchrist Stuart,

Quizzical looks between Peck and Hayward in Paris en route to the "Snows of Kilimanjaro"

Karam Dhaliwal, Aly Wassil, John Farrow, Richard Peel, Aram Katcher, Alberto Morin, Alan Lee, Maurice Colbourne, Tom Cound, Gavin Muir, Pat Whyte, Ramsey Hill. *Prod:* Frank P. Rosenberg for 20th Century-Fox. 99m. Technicolor. CinemaScope. Previous version (*The Black Watch*) 1929 (*dir:* John Ford).

UNTAMED (1955). Action adventure of the Boers in South Africa; location shooting. *Sc:* Talbot Jennings, Frank Fenton, Michael Blankfort (novel by Helga Moray). *Ph:* Leo Tover. *Art dir:* Lyle R. Wheeler, Addison Hehr. *Ed:* Barbara McLean. *Music:* Franz Waxman. *With* Tyrone Power (*Paul Van Riebeck*), Susan Hayward (*Katie O'Neill*), Agnes Moorehead (*Aggie*), Richard Egan (*Kurt*), Rita Moreno (*Julia*), John Justin (*Shawn Kildare*), Hope Emerson (*Maria de Groot*), Brad

Dexter, Henry O'Neill, Paul Thompson, Alexander Havemann, Louis Mercier, Emmett Smith, Jack Macy, Trude Wyler, Louis Polliman Brown, Kevin Corcoran, Brian Corcoran, Tina Thompson, Linda Lowell, Gary Diamond, Bobby Diamond, Ed Mundy, Christian Pasques, Eleanor Audley, Charles Evans, Alberto Morin, Philip Van Zandt, John Dodsworth, Robert Adler, John Carlyle. *Prod:* Bert E. Friedlob and William A. Bacher for 20th Century-Fox. 111m. Colour by De Luxe. CinemaScope.

LOVE IS A MANY-SPLENDORED THING (1955). The love of a Eurasian lady doctor and American war correspondent; location shooting in Hong Kong. *Sc:* John Patrick (novel by Han Suyin). *Ph:* Leon Shamroy. *Art dir:* Lyle R. Wheeler, George W. Davis. *Ed:* William Reynolds. *Music:* Alfred Newman. *With* Jennifer Jones (*Han Suyin*), William Holden (*Mark Elliott*), Torin Thatcher (*Mr. Palmer-Jones*), Isobel Elsom (*Adeline Palmer-Jones*), Murray Matheson (*Dr. Tam*), Virginia Gregg (*Ann Richards*), Richard Loo, Soo Yong, Philip Ahn, Jorja Curtright, Donna Martell, Candace Lee, Kam Tong, James Hong, Herbert Heyes, Angela Loo, Barbara Jean Wong, Marie Tsien, Eleanor Moore, Hazel Shon, Kei Chung. *Prod:* Buddy Adler for 20th Century-Fox. 102m. Colour by De Luxe. CinemaScope.

CAROUSEL (1956). Whimsical romantic musical with elements of fantasy in the life (and death) of fairground barker Billy Bigelow. *Sc:* Phoebe and Henry Ephron (the musical play with book and lyrics by Oscar Hammerstein II, deriving from the play "Liliom" by Ferenc Molnar, as adapted by Benjamin F. Glazer). *Ph:* Charles G. Clarke. *Art dir:* Lyle R. Wheeler, Jack Martin Smith. *Ed:* William Reynolds. *Music:* Richard Rodgers (*dir:* Alfred Newman). *With* Gordon MacRae (*Billy Bigelow*), Shirley Jones (*Julie Jordan*), Cameron Mitchell (*Jigger*), Barbara Ruick (*Carrie*), Claramae Turner (*Cousin Nettie*), Robert Rounseville (*Mr. Snow*), Gene Lockhart (*The Starkeeper*), Audrey Christie (*Mrs. Mullin*), Susan Luckey (*Louise*), Jacques D'Amboise (*Her Dancing Partner*), Frank Tweddell, William Le Massena, Richard Deacon, John Dehner, Dee Pollock, Sylvia Stanton, Ed Mundy, Mary Orozco, Tor Johnson, Harry 'Duke' Johnson, Marion Dempsey, Angelo Rossitto. *Prod:* Henry Ephron for 20th Century-Fox. 128m. Colour by De Luxe. CinemaScope 55. Previous versions of *Liliom*—1930 (*dir:* Frank Borzage) and 1934 (*dir:* Fritz Lang).

THE SUN ALSO RISES (1957). Classic novel of American expatriates, their lives and loves; locations in Europe and Mexico. *Bullfights dir:* Miguel Delgado. *Sc:* Peter Viertel (novel by Ernest Hemingway). *Ph:* Leo Tover. *Art dir:* Lyle R. Wheeler, Mark-Lee Kirk. *Ed:* William Mace. *Music:* Hugo Friedhofer, Alexander Courage. *Music dir:* Lionel Newman. *With* Tyrone Power (*Jake Barnes*), Ava Gardner (*Lady Brett Ashley*), Mel Ferrer (*Robert Cohn*), Errol Flynn (*Mike Campbell*), Eddie Albert (*Bill Gorton*), Gregory Ratoff (*Count Mippipopulous*), Juliette Greco (*Georgette*), Marcel Dalio, Henry Daniell, Bob Cunningham, Robert Evans, Eduardo Noriega, Danik Patisson, Jacqueline Evans, Carlos Muz-

Tyrone Power (far left), Ava Gardner and Eddie Albert in THE SUN ALSO RISES

quiz, Rebecca Iturbi, Carlos David Ortigos. *Prod:* Darryl F. Zanuck for 20th Century-Fox. 129m. Colour by De Luxe. CinemaScope.

THE BRAVADOS (1958). Raw but humane Western concerning a man's revenge on his wife's murderers and the effect on his own personality of such an obsession. *Sc:* Philip Yordan (novel by Frank O'Rourke). *Ph:* Leon Shamroy. *Art dir:* Lyle R. Wheeler, Mark Lee Kirk. *Ed:* William Mace. *Music:* Lionel Newman. *With* Gregory Peck (*Jim Douglas*), Joan Collins (*Josefa Velarde*), Stephen Boyd (*Bill Zachary*), Albert Salmi (*Ed Taylor*), Henry Silva (*Lujan*), Kathleen Gallant (*Emma*), Lee Van Cleef (*Alfonso Parral*), Barry Coe, George Voskovec, Herbert Rudley, Ken Scott, Andrew Duggan, Gene Evans, The Ninos Cantores De Morelia Choral Group, Jack Mather, Joe De Rita, Robert Adler, Jason Wingreen, Robert Griffin, Ada Carrasco, Juan Garcia, Jacqueline Evans, Alicia del Lago. *Prod:* Herbert B. Swope Jr. for 20th Century-Fox. 98m. Colour by De Luxe. CinemaScope.

THIS EARTH IS MINE (1959). Romantic drama with some typical sexual innuendoes of the decade, set among the Californian vineyards. *Sc:* Casey Robinson (novel "The Cup and the Sword" by Alice Tisdale Hobart). *Ph:* Russell Metty, Winton C. Hoch. *Art dir:* Alexander Golitzen, Eric Orbom, George B. Davis. *Ed:* Ted J. Kent. *Music:* Hugo Friedhofer. *With* Jean Simmons (*Elizabeth*), Rock Hudson (*John Rambeau*), Dorothy McGuire (*Martha Fairon*), Claude Rains (*Philippe Rambeau*), Kent Smith (*Francis Fairon*), Anna Lee (*Charlotte Rambeau*), Ken Scott, Cindy Robbins, Augusta Merighi, Francis Bethencourt, Stacy Graham, Peter Chong, Geraldine Wall, Alberto Morin, Penny Santon, Jack Mather, Ben Astor, Daniel White, Lawrence Ung, Ford Dunhill. *Exec. prod:* Edward Muhl. *Prod:* Casey Robinson, Claude Heilman (A Vintage Production for Universal-International release). 125m. Technicolor. CinemaScope.

BELOVED INFIDEL (1959). The tragic romance of Scott Fitzgerald and Sheilah Graham, with an interestingly observed Hollywood background. *Sc:* Sy Bartlett (book by Sheilah Graham and Gerold Frank). *Ph:* Leon Shamroy. *Art dir:* Lyle R. Wheeler, Maurice Ransford. *Ed:* William Reynolds. *Music:* Franz Waxman. *With* Gregory Peck (*F. Scott Fitzgerald*), Deborah Kerr (*Sheilah*

Graham), Eddie Albert (*Carter*), Philip Ober (*John Wheeler*), Herbert Rudley (*Stan Harris*), Karin Booth (*Janet Pierce*), Ken Scott, Buck Class, A. Cameron Grant, John Sutton, Cindy Ames. *Prod:* Jerry Wald for 20th Century-Fox. 123m. Colour by De Luxe. CinemaScope.

TENDER IS THE NIGHT (1961). Fitzgerald's novel based on his own marriage to the beautiful but unstable Zelda. *Sc:* Ivan Moffat (novel by F. Scott Fitzgerald). *Ph:* Leon Shamroy. *Art dir:* Jack Martin Smith, Malcolm Brown. *Ed:* William Reynolds. *Music:* Bernard Herrmann. *With* Jennifer Jones (*Nicole Diver*), Jason Robards Jr. (*Dick Diver*), Joan Fontaine (*Baby Warren*), Tom Ewell (*Abe North*), Cesare Danova (*Tommy Barban*), Jill St. John (*Rosemary Hoyt*), Paul Lukas (*Dr. Dohmler*), Sanford Meisner, Bea Benaderet, Mac McWhorter, Albert Carrier, Richard de Combray, Carole Mathews, Alan Napier, Charles Fredericks, Leslie Farrell, Michael Crisalli, Earl Grant, Maurice Dallinore, Carol Veazie, Arlette Clark. *Prod:* Henry T. Weinstein for 20th Century-Fox. 146m. Colour by De Luxe. CinemaScope.

NOTE: THIS EARTH IS MINE at Universal was King's first film for other than Fox since 1930. In 1963 he prepared a property entitled THE PROMISED LAND at Warners but this was abandoned.

My thanks are due for advice and encouragement to several friends and colleagues in Toronto, especially Patricia Thompson and Glen Hunter. I shall not be the first writer to have cause also to thank William K. Everson of New York. Preparation of the filmography was given a head start by the private researches of Peter Poles, a film history detective of the first order. Additional material prepared by Kingsley Canham, with the assistance of Robert Holton.

Peck, posse, and framing tree in THE BRAVADOS

Milestone: The Unpredictable Fundamentalist

The latter half of the Fifties proved to be a key era in the history of Hollywood. It was a significant turning point in that it marked the end of the "golden years of Hollywood"; the gigantic star factory that raised, nurtured and finally devoured the glittering idols of the screen had begun to crumble at the beginning of the decade under pressure from the spreading popularity of television, and the hysterical publicity which arose from the investigation into Hollywood folk by the Committee of Un-American Activities: adverse publicity that stopped many careers dead, and sent others into exile or "ghost" work. The studio combines began to tighten their purse strings as it became apparent that star names were no longer a guarantee of box-office success. Gimmicks and technical modifications such as 3D, CinemaScope and Cinerama gave rise to more teething troubles than had been anticipated (although none was a new invention). The production lines fell back on cycles of horror and gangster films, while there was also a rise in musicals starring current singing idols like Elvis Presley, Pat Boone and Tommy Sands. But the vanishing faces outnumbered the newcomers.

This was as true of directors as it was of actors and actresses. A sudden change in policy opened the film studio doors to new directors from television, and the established professionals who had become more or less house directors at various studios suddenly found the cold wind of change blowing in their direction. Some like Douglas Sirk or William Wellman retired; the mavericks like Sam Fuller or Don Siegel managed to ride the storm by finding work as independents or occasionally working on TV productions, while others like Tay Garnett, Mitchell Leisen and Lewis Milestone moved almost exclusively into television production.

Emil Jannings and Lewis Milestone on set during THE BETRAYAL

An editorial in the December 1962 issue of "Films and Filming" summed up the critical disposition towards Milestone in discussing the imminent release of his version of *Mutiny on the Bounty*: "In common with so many of the other Old Guard directors, Lewis Milestone's reputation has somewhat tarnished over the last decade. His films no longer bear that stamp of individuality which distinguishes his early work. Milestone of the *Mutiny*, though, is dealing once more with the reactions of men in difficult or dangerous circumstances, a group experience, which has formed the basis of his most compelling work. Called onto the production late, after two other directors had relinquished the assignment, he found a dispirited unit who had spent months sitting around the South Pacific battling the elements—both natural and human—which threatened to turn the entire location into an expensive fiasco . . . It is sixteen years since Milestone last achieved complete success. There have been flashes of his former brilliance, but nothing since *A Walk in the Sun* has achieved stylistic unity."

The use of the phrase "stylistic unity" in the context of Milestone's films has taken on an unfortunate meaning. Time and again his career has been written off because of his lack of commitment to or involvement in his work; the criticism refers to his constant return to war films of admittedly variable quality, yet it ignores both the fact that his career reached a decisive point in the middle and late Thirties when he had established himself as a professional film-maker in every sense, as well as projects like *The Front Page* and *Of Mice and Men* which could not have been dealt with so efficiently had the director not been involved or committed. The lesser stature of some of his work in the mid- and late Thirties must be seen in perspective: Milestone worked on a number of projects which were never filmed, probably taking on assignments from the studios, as did many directors at the time just to keep working since the industry was renowned for its short memory. He has constantly reiterated that he responded to the books that he had a *chance* to film, underlining his insistence on adequate dramatisation of material (thus he worked on nearly every script he filmed without credit in most instances) and his interest in finding economical visual expression for material. He has perhaps over-used the lateral tracking shot, but otherwise he maintains a solid technical level in his handling of players, their dialogue, editing and visual effects, unlike many another director who would leave the camera set-ups to his cinematographer while he waited impatiently to shoot the day's quota of takes.

Lewis Milestone was born in the Ukraine near Odessa, on September 30, 1895. His formal education took place in Russia, but then his parents sent him to a German engineering school in Mitweide, Saxony; the urge to travel proved stronger than his interest in his studies, so the enterprising young man used his return fare home at the end of a term to emigrate to New York. The story goes that on arrival he was financed by an aunt, but ran out of funds; a cable to his father resulted in the following reply: "You are in the land of liberty and labour, so use your own judgement."

He began work as a factory sweeper, then became a salesman and finally a photographic assistant. The latter job stood him in good stead when he enlisted in the U.S. Signal Corps in 1917, since he was assigned as an assistant in the making of army training films. He left the army in 1919, and headed for Hollywood where he found employment as a cutter with Jesse Hampton, an ex-army buddy who had established himself as an independent producer. The following year, Milestone was promoted to the role of general assistant to Henry King, who was working on a two picture contract with Hampton. For the next six years, Milestone took on jobs in any capacity available: he assisted William Seiter, wrote scenarios and treatments and did some editing until he was given the chance to direct a Marie Prevost vehicle.

Mordaunt Hall gave the film, *Seven Sinners* (1925), a moderate but favourable notice in the "New York Times": "This picture is quite diverting and it would have been even better if the humor were lighter in some sequences, and if a touch of satire had been included at the finish. It is the best feature exhibited at Warners for several weeks." Miss Prevost had been a Sennett comedienne; thus she was used to a rapid shooting schedule and Warners and Milestone capitalised by finishing a second comedy vehicle for release two months later. This was *The Cave Man* (1926), about a socialite who introduces her coalman into society with obvious complications such as the coal horses that follow their monkey-suited master along Park Avenue so persistently that he has to climb aboard and drive them to their depot in his top hat and tails! Contemporary reviewers lavished praise on Milestone's adroit direction, and his ability to switch from sophisticated comedy through slapstick to suspense! However they were not so happy about his third feature, *The New Klondike* (1926), a sporting drama based on a story by Ring Lardner. He appears to have been hampered by a predictable script, and a boringly over-virtuous hero, played by Thomas Meighan, then a matinee idol. Still, the fact that it was shot on location in Florida gives some indication of Milestone's rising status as a director.

He only made one film during 1927, but it proved to be his most important silent work. He had left Warner Brothers after the Prevost pictures, working under several banners for the next few years, one of which was the Caddo Company, owned by a rich industrialist with a passion for flying and films, Howard Hughes. His first picture for Hughes was *Two Arabian Knights*, starring William Boyd, Mary Astor and Louis Wolheim. It was Milestone's first war film, inasmuch as it dealt with the comical adventures of two American doughboys, who escape from a German prison camp during the First World War, and accidentally wind up in the Middle East where they bicker over an Arabian girl, and take on a gang of cut-throats, headed by her father.

Obviously, it was made to cash in on the popularity of Raoul Walsh's *What Price Glory* (1926), for the relationships between the central characters were identical, and the two films also shared one of the writers, James T. O'Donohue. Whereas Walsh's film won plaudits for an earthy, rugged humour, Milestone's relied on intelligent acting at the expense of any slapstick comedy, a quality

Thomas Meighan (third from left) in THE RACKET

which helped win him the Academy Award for best direction. Hughes's company had a releasing agreement with United Artists, who also distributed Milestone's next film, *The Garden of Eden* (1928), which was produced by John W. Considine Jr. A brilliant Oxford graduate, Considine was chosen by Hughes as his production supervisor, and was later to become a successful producer in his own right at M-G-M. *The Garden of Eden* was a comedy-drama, written by one of Ernst Lubitsch's favourite writers, Hans Kraly, and once more Milestone's deft direction of players enhanced the often acidic sophistication of his material. Possibly to avoid type-casting as a comedy director, he changed pace with his third picture for Hughes, *The Racket* (1928), a gutty drama of gang-war and political corruption, which reunited him with Louis Wolheim.

Like Victor McLaglen, Wolheim has tended to be classed as a "one show" actor, repeating his performance as a hulking brute, but this is probably another myth of film history since his performance as a ruthless beer baron engaged in a struggle to the death with a rival bootlegger was, by all accounts, sympathetic and controlled. Although praised for its technical virtues (an intelligent use of half-lighting; camera placement and a solid integration of movement and tension), *The Racket's* reception was marred by a release date amid a plethora of similar gangster films of variable quality. However the subject remained a favourite project for Howard Hughes who produced a sound re-make in 1951, directed by John Cromwell.

While *The Racket* had played down the love interest to good advantage, Milestone's remaining silent film, *The Betrayal* (1929), and his first talkie, *New York Nights* (1929), both concentrated on it, partially to their detriment. The former, which marked the last silent appearances of Gary Cooper and Emil Jannings, was a hopelessly archaic piece of Alpine corn, with Cooper miscast as an artist who fathers an illegitimate baby before leaving for the city, only to discover the truth on his return. He attempts to come between the mother and her newly acquired husband, the mayor, with tragic results. Once more Milestone was allowed the freedom of location shooting for some sequences, but all the village scenes were shot in cramped studio conditions, resulting in stilted, obviously false images. *New York Nights* was a highly dramatic gangster piece, scripted by Jules Furthman, and photographed by Ray June, but it gave little indication of Milestone's ability in adapting to sound techniques.

Thus Milestone ended the silent period with a good record of achievement; within five years of directing he had won one Oscar, and one of his pictures (*The Racket*) had been nominated as a picture of the year; critically he was acknowledged as a sound technician and inventive comedy director while commercially his films had been successful in spite of a slight falling off in quality during the last year of the decade. But he realised he had to make his mark quickly as a sound director.

Luckily, he had one of the smartest agents in the business, David O. Selznick's brother Myron. Myron Selznick heard of plans to film Erich Maria Remarque's best-selling novel *All Quiet on the Western Front* at Universal. The studio head, Carl Laemmle, had grown up with the cinema from the early days, and was one of many to hold the opinion that sound was a flash-in-the-pan fad. He had given his son, Junior, the job of head of studio production as a twenty-first birthday present. Junior immediately announced a major change in policy: in future the company would move away from simple, family entertainment to make big pictures with challenging themes, and he selected Remarque's work to set the ball rolling. The film eventually cost 1,250,000 dollars, and had many teething problems before the cameras eventually began rolling.

Herbert Brenon was selected as director, but was dropped when he asked for a fee of 125,000 dollars, which the elder Laemmle considered excessive. Overtures were also unsuccessfully made to Paul Fejos, at which point Myron Selznick entered the field, offering Milestone's services for a fee of five thousand dollars a week over a minimum of ten weeks with a pro rata fee if shooting took longer. He had foreseen the type of delays which might arise on

Opposite: Milestone (on boom with cigar) directing Lew Ayres and Raymond Griffith in ALL QUIET ON THE WESTERN FRONT

a project of this scale, and thereby netted his client a final salary of 135,000 dollars since the preparation of the script took ten weeks, and the shooting occupied another seventeen weeks. It was originally planned as a silent film, and in fact two versions, one silent and one sound were shot on location at the Irving Ranch, about fifty miles from Hollywood, and at Universal Studios and Balboa, almost unique since they were shot largely *in sequence*.

Milestone was unhappy with the original script, prepared by Maxwell Anderson, which he felt pared down and changed the scope and point of Remarque's book, so he engaged a friend Del Andrews (who had originally taught him cutting) with whom he threshed out the rough outline of the existing film. Anderson accepted Milestone's ideas, and was re-assigned to write the dialogue, although he retained credit in collaboration for the screenplay. The writing team was completed by George Abbott, a well-known stage director, who was brought in at a later stage to shape the final script. Milestone also supervised the casting, resisting Junior's suggestion of James Murray (the unknown actor who gave a brilliant performance in King Vidor's *The Crowd*, but then vanished into oblivion and an early death) for the role of the hard-bitten, professional soldier, Katczinsky, in favour of his old friend and colleague, Louis Wolheim. He searched fruitlessly for an unknown actor to play Paul, the leading role, until Myron Selznick (probably worried about his investment!) suggested the hiring of a dialogue director to assist with the casting. His choice was George Cukor, who not only became a firm friend to Milestone, but also discovered the leading man. A few days before shooting was due to commence, Cukor was running tests for Milestone who was suddenly struck by the self-possessed dignity of a young actor named Lew Ayres. He met the young man, and knew his search was over: ironically, Ayres had been trying to contact Milestone through mutual acquaintances for some weeks

A soldier's training: ALL QUIET ON THE WESTERN FRONT

without success, so in desperation he had turned up at the studio to test for a role in the film.

Junior proved a reasonable producer, normally leaving Milestone to have the last say on the production, although he had to be talked out of changing Lew Ayres's name (Ayres was under twenty-one and theoretically had no say in the matter), and there was some dissension between him and Milestone over the ending of the film. Both disliked the original ending of the book in which Paul dies heroically, but neither could suggest an alternative acceptable to both parties, until Karl Freund, the famous cameraman, put forward the idea of the hand stretching out toward

79

the butterfly. Milestone shot the take the following day, filming his own hand instead of that of Lew Ayres's, and a preview print was prepared. The showing went very well until Zasu Pitts appeared as Paul's mother; typecasting had long associated her with comedy parts (in spite of leading dramatic roles in Stroheim's *Greed* and *The Wedding March*) with the result that her every appearance created laughter. She had to be replaced with Beryl Mercer, an archetypal screen mother, who thankfully was not allowed to repeat her excesses of a similar role in Richard Wallace's *Seven Days Leave* the previous year.

Milestone's film was not the first to examine the Great War from the German point of view [cf. John Ford's *Four Sons* (1928)], but it was one of the few to do so with impartiality. The locale was totally convincing, unlike many later efforts, and the script wisely chose to concentrate upon the effects of war on individual characters, instead of making wordy statements about the nature of war. The pattern of the editing was linked to the style of writing and filming (i.e. fast cutting for the early shots in which seven recruits join the Kaiser's army, bounding with enthusiasm and patriotism—at the instigation of the local school-master), which avoids all the "blood and guts through hell to glory" *clichés* by taking a starkly realistic look at death—meted out by shelling, shrapnel, bayonets, barbed wire and a sniper's bullet.

The recruits find army discipline is not the temporary affair of the class-room; nor is the dislike of the ex-village postman something which they can ignore or avoid as he is now their superior. Interestingly, this class motif reappears in Douglas Sirk's film about the Second World War, *A Time to Love and a Time to Die* (1958), when the hero, Ernst Graeber, returns from the Russian front on leave, and in the course of his search for his parents who have been bombed out of their home, encounters an old school-mate of humble origins, who has raised himself "socially" by embracing the Nazi philosophy. But in Sirk's film there is no antipathy between the two men; instead the Nazi official is shown as being lonely and eager to seek Graeber's companionship.

Milestone's recruits meet their final disillusion with their first experience of the front lines; they are horrified by the sight of the troop trains spilling out the wounded from every crevice, or the battlefields covered with the dead and dying as men drop around them like flies. The process of disillusionment is not gradual; on his first leave, Paul Baumer responds to a question about conditions: "We live in the trenches and we fight. We try not to be killed—that's all." *Clichés* such as passing romances or over-emotional death scenes are avoided by low-key performances, with Lew Ayres to the fore. He is beautifully articulate, and his acting deserves to be remembered for other than the vital scenes—the one in the trench with the dying French soldier (Raymond Griffith); the pacifist speech at his school when he returns on leave, and the final shot with the butterfly—scenes like his rage as the boots of a dead comrade are dispassionately removed from the body, or the early sequences in which the recruits get to know the veteran soldiers with whom they have been billeted.

But above all it was the technique of Milestone's film that rightly led to its fame. The movement became the message at a time when talkies were reputed to be static and stagebound because of the problems of adapting photographic needs to the demands of sound recording. The reappearance of many early films which do not fit into this category now suggests that this aspect may have been exaggerated by early sound historians, and certainly Milestone's work is one of these exceptions. One of the most obvious examples is the machine-gun sequence with intercut crane shots of soldiers being mowed down as they try to cross a field, contrasting with still shots of the guns reaping their harvest of death. The visual effect is linked to the staccato soundtrack of the firing guns, thus heightening the intensity. The high quality of Milestone's directorial abilities had opened up a broad spectrum of opportunity for him, but the pitfalls of fame and the studio system were not to be forgotten.

Milestone's persistence in finding material that could be adequately dramatised was rewarded in *The Front Page,* the famous Hecht-MacArthur play about the unethical behaviour of scandal-seeking pressmen. The action was driven along at a cracking pace, backed by sparkling dialogue and excellent acting by Pat O'Brien and Adolphe Menjou. Probably the most famous of all newspaper dramas, its hard, fast and ruthless pace also contained oblique references to the political and press chicaneries of the period—but not as amorally shaded as Wellman's *Love Is a Racket* (1932). Milestone's control of dialogue and performances set a new "house standard" for Warner Brothers (cf. the similar pace, dialogue and acting style in Michael Curtiz's *Jimmy the Gent,* made in 1934) and also sparked off a cycle of newspaper films such as *Five Star Final, Blessed Event* and *It Happened One Night,* but the original play proved such a successful entity in itself that he was unable to impose much of himself on his material. The visual signature of the long tracking shot is there at the opening, with a stunning track through the newspaper machine room, and later in the scene of Mae Clark's impassioned speech before her suicide. The camera movement backwards in the latter sequence registers the players' reactions, but it is also open to the interpretation of a Catholic rejection of the act of suicide.

The heavier note struck by the moralising and obvious social comment of the scene is at odds with the double-taking comedy of Clarence Wilson, who steals scenes from such hardened comedy veterans as Edward Everett Horton and Frank McHugh with consummate ease; elsewhere a note of topicality is struck with the racial jokes and the "Red scare" paranoia. The fable introduction and the question mark over the ending as the rascally editor, Walter Burns (Adolphe Menjou), relishes his last trick to retain his star reporter (by giving him a watch as a wedding gift and memento, and then ringing his office to have the New York train stopped by the police: "The son of a bitch stole my watch") are reminders of the sophisticated silent comedies with which Milestone made his name, and underline his absorption of technique. Significantly, Howard Hawks in his celebrated re-make, *His Girl Friday* (1940), toned down the moral issues and opted instead for hilarious black comedy, delivered in even faster verbal assaults! Re-seen today, *The Front Page* earns the just reputation of a Hollywood classic as much from the contributions of the authors and players as from Milestone's direction.

Milestone's new-found reputation as a moralist no doubt led to his being offered *Rain* as his following project. Unfortunately, moral issues in the Hollywood system carried a double edge. Escapism and fantasy proved superior to realism at the box-office, therefore many realistic films were marred by studio imposed insertions of romantic, sentimental or sanctimonious scenes; alternatively naïve plots which had been successful in the past were dragged out for another airing with generally disastrous results. *Rain* was one of the latter.

Somerset Maugham's story about a tart with a heart who falls under the domination of a hypocritical missionary and his stern wife on a South Sea Island had previously been filmed as a silent vehicle for Gloria Swanson by Raoul Walsh in 1928. The theme was rather corny and outdated at that time, but Walsh's robust humour and Swanson's spirited playing had turned it into a commercially successful vehicle. Milestone was given the rising talent of Joan Crawford for his leading lady. As was often the case in the Thirties, the *star* was assigned a role regardless of the nature of the role or of the talent of the star for that particular part. Milestone was definitely courting fate by taking the material completely seriously since the language had to be toned down considerably for a talkie; captions on a silent film could and did cover a multitude of uses with visual *suggestion* substituting for strong verbal passages.

But the talkies had to talk; censorship was fairly lax during the early sound period but language was still tightly restricted; Mae West had not yet shaken the industry with her *double entendres* (if Walsh had directed Mae West in a talkie version of *Rain* the result might have been quite pungent!), and subjects involving the Church had to be handled with kid gloves. The resulting film was slow and stage-bound, enlivened only by the fervour of Walter Huston's bigot. Milestone himself commented: "I thought they [audiences] were ready for a dramatic form; that now we could present a three act play on the screen. But I was wrong. People will not listen to narrative dialogue. They will not accept the kind of exposition you use on the stage. I started the picture slowly, too slowly, I'm afraid. You can't start a picture slowly. You must show things happening."

He struck out again with *Hallelujah, I'm a Bum,* a musical comedy starring Al Jolson and Harry Langdon, from a story by Ben Hecht, and with songs by Rodgers and Hart. The project had been conceived to couple rhyming dialogue and music, but this structure proved too much for the original director, so Milestone was called in. Contemporary reports suggest that Jolson was far from happy with the film, and that it suffered by comparison with Rouben Mamoulian's *Love Me Tonight* (1932), which had also employed this experimental format with the musical assistance of Rodgers and Hart, but also with more impressive production values. At this point in his career, Milestone seemed to be faltering; then came an offer from Alexander Korda in England, suggesting Milestone consider making H. G. Wells's *The Shape of Things to Come*. Unfortunately, negotiations fell through (the film was later made by another American, William Cameron Menzies, in 1936), so Milestone returned to comedy with a ship-board fairy tale starring John Gilbert and Victor McLaglen. *The Captain Hates the Sea* ended Gilbert's fading career; *Paris in Spring* and *Anything Goes* did little for Milestone.

The three latter films were made for Paramount; as a studio it was always in the running with the other major studios although, as John Baxter pointed out in "Hollywood in the Thirties," it was not always as financially sound as some of the others. Paramount's output was a mixed bag, dominated at the top of the scale by the films of Ernst Lubitsch and Cecil B. DeMille, with Leisen, Alexander Hall and Wesley Ruggles in the middle ranks, and Robert Florey for low budget projects. Both Milestone and Rouben Mamoulian remained outside the ranks, probably because they reached certain peaks at a time when the studio was proceeding cautiously through internal financial worries or internal politics. Between 1933 and 1936, Lubitsch was in second gear at Paramount, worked on loan out and spent a year as a production executive, while Josef von Sternberg's exotic works with Marlene Dietrich were at their peak, but the studio was trying to impose on von Sternberg with the end result of a parting of the ways. Thus the strong European influence at Paramount was on a temporary wane, a factor which might be very relevant in assessing Milestone's apparent decline in the mid-Thirties.

However his next film, *The General Died at Dawn*, displayed a marked return to form, and heralded a European revival continued by Lubitsch and Billy Wilder. It was a stylised drama,

J. M. Kerrigan, Porter Hall, Gary Cooper, and Madeleine Carroll in
THE GENERAL DIED AT DAWN

visually as well as thematically reminiscent of von Sternberg's *Shanghai Express*. Oddly Milestone himself does not care too much for the film, as he considered the source to be negligible; he has often played down his part in achieving visual expression, preferring to stress points about acting and writing:

"I do my figuring on paper instead of doing it on film. It bores me to do the same scene just to get another angle. I generally work out a storyboard with a sketch artist. But my storyboards are born as a result of careful rehearsals. The sketches serve as memoranda. On *All Quiet* I tried this method with one sequence. It worked like a charm. The mechanical side of film-making was out of my way and I could concentrate on performances. That's the way I worked from that point on."

The effortless ease and economy with which he sketches the Gary Cooper character at the start of *The General Died at Dawn* by involving him in a confrontation with a stupid, loud-mouthed American couple; the skill of the script as it weaves a tangle of snares for the characters whom it has trapped between opposing social forces; and the acting itself combine to lift it out of the main stream of adventure pictures that utilised the inscrutable Orient as a backdrop. The latter quality obscures the impact of the first symphonic musical score composed for a film; the bravura camera techniques such as split screen images or a dissolve match cut from a billiard ball to a white door knob. The biggest impact is in Madeleine Carroll's portrayal of Judy Perrie as a frightened lost girl; her efforts to aid her consumptive father by working for a warlord set up a series of vibrations, rather like the effect of tossing a stone into a pool with the resultant ripple of circles on the surface. Duplicity and deceptive appearances abound in Milestone's films in various forms: the innocence of the recruits going to war in *All Quiet,* only to be shattered by their first experiences at the front; the satirical commentary on pleasure cruises in *The Captain Hates the Sea* that suddenly smacks of seriousness when it involves a suicide attempt and the shooting of a revolutionary; the young English sailor in *Kangaroo* who poses as a long-lost son of a rich station owner in order to rob him, but develops a conscience when he falls in love with the man's daughter; or the childhood secret that binds the lives of the three leading characters in *The Strange Love of Martha Ivers.*

The success of *The General Died at Dawn* should have revitalised Milestone's career; instead he found himself involved in a series of unfulfilled projects that kept his work off the screen for three years. Censorship prevented him from filming Vincent Shee-han's *Personal History* for Walter Wanger; Sam Goldwyn commissioned him and Clifford Odets to write a screenplay for *Dead End,* but then turned the project over to William Wyler, while in 1938 Hal Roach asked him to film a project entitled *Road Show.* After Milestone had done some initial work on a screenplay, Roach shelved the project for two years, when he directed it himself. Eventually Paramount offered him a show business story, *The Night of Nights,* about a playwright who ruins his career by appearing drunk and disorderly at the first night of his play. His wife leaves him, and subsequently dies but many years later his daughter triumphs in a revival of the play, leaving her father to die a contented man. Although contemporary critics praised the skill with which Milestone moved from humour to tragedy without any flippancy, and the honesty of the sequences where father and daughter come to an understanding of one another, the film is very infrequently shown today, and was merely a stand-by piece that Milestone filmed solely to keep working.

Hal Roach gave Milestone a break by asking him to film John Steinbeck's *Of Mice and Men* on a small budget and a rapid shooting schedule. It has been suggested that the timing and haste of the project stemmed from a desire to cash in on the possible success of *The Grapes of Wrath,* which John Ford had begun preparing at this time, but if this was true the scheme failed as the Milestone film met with considerable critical success but failed at the box-office. In any event it restored Milestone's reputation as an outstanding technician: the economy of the opening sequence as two men flee from a posse behind the credits set an example that was reconstituted by Arthur Penn in *The Chase,* which was in many ways a more complex re-working of Milestone's work; controlled camera movement in both films gave a depth of spatial relation-

Burgess Meredith and Lon Chaney Jr. in OF MICE AND MEN

ship to both foreground and background action. Precise editing in *Of Mice and Men* discarded conventional overlaps, while stylised acting (as in *Rain*, a similar sort of morality play) underlined the conflict of the characters and their situation, and was well served by the combined talents of Lon Chaney Jr. in his only major role in an "A" film as the halfwit Lennie, Burgess Meredith as his "keeper" George, and Betty Field as the stupid, faithless farmer's wife who causes the tragedy. Yet again the score, one of several composed for Milestone by Aaron Copland, played a decisive role

Olin Howland, Ronald Colman, and Ginger Rogers in
LUCKY PARTNERS

in the form of the film: natural sounds and dialogue sequences
were interpolated with the music to act as complementary *motif*
to the visual and narrative development.

A two picture deal with RKO offered Milestone a double
comedy package with Ronald Colman as star and John Van Druten
as co-scripter. Both films were adapted from French source material;
Lucky Partners, from a Sacha Guitry story, co-starred Colman with
Ginger Rogers, who was trying quite successfully at the time to
prove her acting ability after a string of musicals with Fred Astaire.

90

Colman is an artist with a shady past, posing as a cartoonist, who wins a raffle draw with Rogers and takes her to Niagara Falls for a platonic honeymoon! The second, and more successful, comedy was a frothy, totally disarming frolic entitled *My Life with Caroline*, featuring Colman as a whimsical New York publisher, who narrates in flashback how he saved his wife (Anna Lee) from precipitate elopements with her sympathetic admirers, including Reginald Gardiner and Gilbert Roland.

Milestone returned to the subject of war with a documentary, *Our Russian Front*, which he co-produced with Joris Ivens and edited, before embarking on the first of three films written for him by Robert Rossen. Warner Brothers had offered them a one film contract with Errol Flynn as star; they began work on a version of *Moby Dick*, but the project fell through, so they put together a war story about the Norwegian underground, *Edge of Darkness*. True to form, Milestone opened the film with a stunning impact, investing the set formula of the Hollywood propaganda movie with a new vigour and depth, yet with a customary economy of imagery. The camera moves in on a small Norwegian port, flying the Norwegian flag. Dead Germans and Norwegians lie everywhere; the only living soul is a babbling lunatic. This method of anti-suspense, later used by Sirk in melodramas, gives way to a flashback leading up to and continuing beyond the opening shot.

His next project, *The North Star*, was produced by Samuel Goldwyn, and was written by Lillian Hellman, and this too was in the tradition of the Hollywood propaganda movie of the period in that it used Russia as a background to the action, favouring the characters with a sympathetic presentation; in later years this approach became somewhat of an embarrassment, and a re-issue print entitled *Armored Attack* carried a doctored soundtrack with anti-Communist material being overlaid. But even without this addition, the film does not stand comparison with other Hollywood

Ann Sheridan, Tom Fadden, and Errol Flynn in
EDGE OF DARKNESS

"Russian" films as it tends to linger on the horrors of the Nazi invasion. The script works on the basis of force and simplicity, but the film surprisingly fails in the translation of emotional tension into visual images (e.g. the peasants moving across the plains in slow wagons, looking apprehensively at the bright, blank sky as the first of the German bombers are heard, or the girl who turns away from the blinded boy as he asks her if it is day or night emerge as banalities or superfluous, predictable images).

Occasionally, in instances such as the subtle use of silence, or in the technical precision of the composition of the movement of men and horses across the screen during a guerilla attack, Milestone's professionalism transcends his material, and there is one especially memorable shot of a look that passes over a peasant woman's face as she lights a lamp in preparation for setting her home alight that strikes the viewer with the impact of true Hollywood expertise (e.g. the woman in Fritz Lang's *Fury* brandishing the burning cloth as she riots with the mob outside the prison). These war projects did relate to a structural aspect of Milestone's work: the group reacting under pressure, but his later war efforts were far more coherent in developing this framework within a personal viewpoint.

The Purple Heart was another studio property which dealt with an isolated incident. It laid stress on the dialogue and on character, but was marred by jingoistic propaganda inserts. An atmospheric opening has the camera prowling around a deserted courtroom as an orderly enters, switches on the light and tidies up. The camera settles briefly on the flag of the Rising Sun before invited foreign journalists arrive. The Russian and Portuguese representatives are barred ("Please to refer complaints to the Bureau of Enlightenment"). They have been given no indication as to the nature of the summons, and are surprised to find that it is a civil court; they also speculate as to the presence of top Army and Navy officers, and of one of the foremost judges. Eight American fliers are led in (to the strains of "The Wild Blue Yonder"), and are formally arraigned ("The charge? You will be informed later!").

They are assigned a lawyer, who smilingly informs them that he is Princeton educated—class of '31. The barrack-room lawyer amongst them, Greenbaum (Sam Levene), quotes the Geneva Convention, so the judge reveals the charge—murder of women and children through indiscriminate bombing. Two witnesses are called: the Chinese governor who handed them over to the Japs when their plane crashed in his province, and a General who shows fake film of their alleged crime. No right of cross-examination is allowed unless the judge doubts the integrity of a witness. The day's proceedings end with a murder in the court, and a cat and mouse game begins as the prisoners are locked in a cage. The ever prowling camera increases the tension while the men wait and discuss their situation, and personal reaction to torture. They are tortured, but in such a way that they do not know who will be next, or what form the torture will take—so that they all crowd around the youngest man (Farley Granger), asking him questions, until they realise that his tongue has been cut off; another man (Richard Conte) seems unmarked until he moves his arms to show that both wrists have been broken . . .

A sub-plot shows the political rivalry between the General and an Admiral, both anxious to lay the blame for the bombing raids on each other; when the General makes his point he offers to have the charges withdrawn but the Americans cannot meet his condition and go proudly to their deaths as the strains of "The Wild Blue Yonder" swamps the soundtrack. The subplot is pivotal in accepting Milestone's attitude towards war as it indicates a change in heart from his pacifist position of *All Quiet on the Western Front*. The claustrophobic atmosphere, and the suspense generated during the opening sequences are maintained throughout, and the acting is uniformly good with the American fliers representing an international cross-section of characters as was usual in films of this sort. Arthur Miller's photography used crisp, clearly defined, high-key images for the court scenes, and contrastingly low-key imagery for a flashback to the capture of the fliers, and again Milestone relied heavily on natural sound.

A Walk in the Sun synthesised his reappraisal of men in war. The plot was sparse, but tightly constructed in a series of episodes (all containing an underlying melancholia). The dialogue was deliberately stylised: repetition, catch phrases and obsessional figures of speech produced an effect of blank verse, the rhythm of which heightened the sense of fear and isolation, and they were accompanied by a ballad singer on the soundtrack (pre-dating *High Noon*). The camerawork was muted throughout; sound and silence were deliberately juxtaposed with sudden bursts of action punctuating the narrative (e.g. the beachhead landing in darkness, the bomb attack or the final assault on the farm-house).

Dana Andrews and a dying Sterling Holloway in
A WALK IN THE SUN

Character was to the fore in the acting but, unlike a Flynn film, there was no set hero or mock heroics. Instead a number of soldiers move in and out of the narrative baring their likes, dislikes and their hopes and fears; some return while others are seen only once, and many die. Dana Andrews as Sergeant Tyne, the man who never liked to travel; Richard Conte as Riviera, the Italian-American machine-gunner who loved opera, and wanted a pretty wife and many children; George Tyne as Friedman, the lathe operator and amateur boxer; John Ireland as Windy, the minister's son who likes to walk alone and think; Sterling Holloway as Mc-Williams, the slow but dependable first aid man; and Norman Lloyd's sour prophet with his prediction that they will still be fighting in 1958, probably around Tibet, represent more than just a knot of men in war.

They are a group of unwilling civilians, who find themselves at war in a strange land. They also imply a structural and moral change in Milestone's attitude by their tacit acceptance of the conditions of war. As one of the characters says: "We've got a grandstand seat, only we can't see nothing. That's the trouble with war, you can't see nothing! You have to find them by ear."

A sense of purposelessness pervades the film; a blind serving of a plan whose shape and final outcome means nothing to the men who are fighting the war, and as such it looks forward to *Pork Chop Hill. A Walk in the Sun* was Rossen's second script for Milestone; whereas it can be seen as an integral part of Milestone's vision and style, their last collaboration on *The Strange Love of Martha Ivers* marks the emergence of a personal style on the part of Rossen as certain of his interests and concerns from his later work are apparent.

Milestone had not worked on a full-blooded "woman's melodrama" for many years after *Rain*, although this was not really in the same vein as the later Crawford vehicles. He shared credit

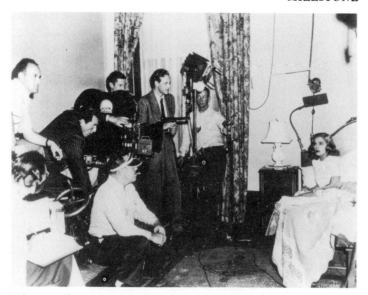

Milestone (leaning on camera) directs Lizabeth Scott in
THE STRANGE LOVE OF MARTHA IVERS.
Third from right is Van Heflin

for some work on *Guest in the House* (1944, John Brahm) which
dealt with the evil influence of an apparently innocent but sick
young lady (Anne Baxter in a dress rehearsal for her outstanding
performance in *All about Eve*) on a doctor's household; but with
The Strange Love of Martha Ivers he undoubtedly gave a sense of
freshness to his material. It became more than a superficial melodrama; the viciousness of dialogue and character reflected a cynical
approach to modern society, and it was elevated to a powerful
demonstration of the destructive distortion of identity in the face

97

of a love which stemmed from an obsessive devotion to money and power.

Casting against type, Milestone used Kirk Douglas as a weak, alcoholic District Attorney, dominated by his ambitious wife, Stanwyck, and Van Heflin (often a weak character) as a childhood friend who returns to town by accident, and becomes involved in Martha's schemes. Douglas is suspicious of him ("He's an angle boy. Can't you see blackmail in his eyes?") when he discovers Heflin has a reputation as a gambler, and tries to put pressure on him to leave town by leaning on a girl (Lizabeth Scott) whom Heflin has befriended. It is a good indication of the normality of the Heflin/Scott relationship that when he finds she has been double-crossing him, his first reaction is to beat the truth out of her! Equally when he confronts Douglas, the polite façade soon erupts into violence with Heflin crushing Douglas's fingers in a drawer as he goes for a gun.

When Douglas begins to level with him, talking about the sense of power ("You get to feel like God"), and when he tells Stanwyck, "You were my life's work," Heflin becomes curious, and plays up to Martha. A fire starts them reminiscing about their childhood, and he detects a strange reference to her aunt; then she attacks him in a highly sexually charged sequence. Violence escalates as Douglas taunts Heflin about his affair with Stanwyck ("You're not the first—her old man forced her!" Heflin: "How long do you expect her to keep paying off?" Douglas: "Forever. Unless you kill her now, you'll be next!"). She in turn urges Heflin to murder Douglas when he falls down the stairs in a drunken fit, but he refrains when he learns that she killed her aunt with Douglas as witness when they were children. Heflin calls her bluff on killing him, and leaves her with Douglas who soothes her ("It's not anyone's fault; it's not the way things are. Just how *hard* people want things."). She responds amorously, and when he produces the gun, she turns it on herself; Heflin returns in time to see Douglas shoot himself, and then leaves to meet Lizabeth Scott with the explanation for his actions throughout the film: "I wanted to see if I could be lucky twice."

The Strange Love of Martha Ivers worked as a melodrama because of a plausible small town background and a well-paced rhythm which point up the succeeding scenes of cruelty, but Milestone's next attempt at melodrama failed badly, although no little blame for the failure lies with Milestone himself. The studio, Universal, was keen to repeat a successful filming of a Remarque novel, but certain studio executives did not like the long version that Milestone turned in, so it was drastically pruned and re-edited, and today Milestone practically disowns *Arch of Triumph.*

He continued to work prolifically, turning out a rarely seen comedy, *No Minor Vices*; his first Technicolor film, an adaptation of John Steinbeck's *The Red Pony*; and then returned to the subject of war with *Halls of Montezuma,* a tale of the Marines featuring Richard Widmark as a neurotic section leader, who suffers from psychological migraine and has to depend on a supply of pills to keep his cool. As in *A Walk in the Sun* and Samuel Fuller's *Fixed Bayonets* the script attempts to examine the qualities of leadership. Flashbacks fill in the civilian lives and problems of the characters, and are quite well integrated; naturalistic sound and lighting predominates, but the film is marred by concessions to sentimentality such as a reading of the Lord's Prayer by Karl Malden before the final battle.

The setting for Milestone's next film for 20th Century-Fox was unusual, but the plot resembled a routine Western format: *Kangaroo* cast Peter Lawford as a sailor who falls in with bad company (Richard Boone), and is persuaded to pass himself off as the long-lost son and heir of an Australian cattle station owner. The problems of identity are confused when he falls in love with his

Finlay Currie in KANGAROO

"sister" (Maureen O'Hara). Milestone's handling of the material was interesting in the extent of carrying sound and lack of dialogue to extremes, but the standard of playing was below par.

Fox loaded his next film with contract players, but again Milestone was working with an indifferent script. *Les Misérables* had been filmed many times before (indeed the plot of *Arch of Triumph* was not without similarities to the Hugo tale), but capable direction and lavish sets and model work helped capture the sense and feeling of the piece. Robert Newton as the policeman, obsessively tracking down a parole violator, Michael Rennie, who has been trying to lead a decent life, is outstanding. His gruff voice and arch over-playing are perfectly suited to delivering lines such as: "If he has escaped us tonight, what of tomorrow, next week, next year?"

Failure at the box-office was not a good omen for an established director, particularly in the Fifties, but Milestone had little success with either of the two films that he made in England. *Melba* was an ill-fated attempt to cash in on the success of the recently filmed

Cameron Mitchell and Michael Rennie in LES MISERABLES

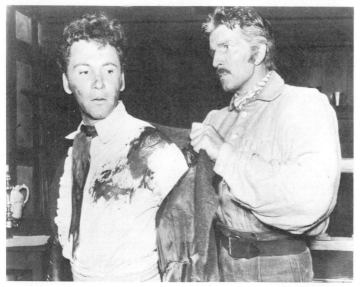

biography of Gilbert and Sullivan; Sam Spiegel produced the film for Milestone but in spite of the presence of Patricia Munsel as Dame Nellie Melba, it turned out to be a disastrous flop. His succeeding film, *They Who Dare*, told of a trial small-scale raid on Luftwaffe bases in Greece. The raiders consisted of a green young officer (Dick Bogarde); a singing Lancashire lad (Sam Kydd); a cynic who shuns any responsibility (Denholm Elliott); and an artist whose rogues' gallery portraits of drawings of Bogarde amuse the officer in charge of the operation.

Milestone introduces the characters and creates a mood of joviality, then jolts their situation into perspective as tension flares at the briefing session when red wine is spilt across the map. After a bloodless landing, they nearly walk into a minefield but are saved at the last moment by a billy-goat. Their luck runs out when a spring runs dry; a Greek guide sent ahead to scout out a village vanishes; one of the group, giving chase, falls to the ground with blood flowing from an old, unhealed wound. Children frighten them into changing hideouts, and they land up in another minefield! They are thoroughly demoralised, and Bogarde nearly calls off the mission, but when food supplies arrive he changes his mind . . .

Apart from occasional lapses in overstatement, and some uneven characterisation, Robert Westerby's script is good. Milestone directs efficiently, calling on his cameraman to provide some beautifully composed night shots, and minimising editing with an economic use of wipes and fades. The fallibility of individuals and their forced adaptation to situations not of their choosing once more replaces the conventional action plot. Indeed, the first death occurs after 92 minutes of the 101 minute running time. The major drawback of the film lies in the casting of Dirk Bogarde, who imbalances his performance with too much physical anger and too little introspection. This tends to stretch credulity when he gains control of himself after lapsing into self-pity, and approaches each incident with single-minded optimism in spite of the increasing gravity of their situation. The film becomes a conventional "miracle" work at this point, for the *clichés* predominate to such an extent that the hero's triumph becomes inevitable, and he becomes more of a mythical creation than a naturalistically observed character.

After an Italian/American co-production starring Patricia Roc, *The Widow,* Milestone turned to television for several years, working on a number of series including *Have Gun, Will Travel* starring his old friend, Richard Boone, but he was tempted back at the end of the decade to direct *Pork Chop Hill,* a Korean war drama with Gregory Peck, who also played a major role in the production of the film. The released version differed from Milestone's original conception in that he had intended to include much more cross-cutting between the action of holding the hill and the peace talks that were going on as the action was played out. He had also intended that the Peck character should be less of the conventional hero since he was again making his point about men fighting blindly for objectives without being aware of the point of their actions or the strategy that lay behind it, but he was not able to have his own way.

The following year he turned out a pedestrian comedy thriller, *Ocean's Eleven,* starring Frank Sinatra and some of his Rat Pack, but the subject matter—a raid on a casino—was much better in the shape of a straight thriller as Henry Hathaway proved with his *Seven Thieves,* which was released at the beginning of the year, taking the edge off Milestone's film. The last film which bears Milestone's name as director was the re-make of *Mutiny on the Bounty,* but it is hardly representative of his work since the final film is reputed to contain scenes shot by George Seaton, Richard Thorpe, Andrew Marton, Billy Wilder, Fred Zinnemann and Marlon Brando among others.

After this fiasco, Milestone returned briefly to television, and then did some preliminary work on *P.T. 109*, the story of the late President John F. Kennedy's war experiences, but he fell out with Jack L. Warner, the film's executive producer, and was replaced by Leslie H. Martinson. Two years later he was announced as director of an episode of *The Secret War*, but once more he was replaced before shooting began. He now lives in retirement in Beverly Hills, a vigorous and outspoken man despite an ailment that has impaired his walking ability.

The superlative craftsmanship of his films has earned him a place in film history; it was quite a feat on his part to remain working at all since he had broken the rules of the game in the earliest days of his career. He revolted against Warner Brothers studio control during the making of the Prevost pictures, and broke his contract. They took him to court and he was made to go through bankruptcy proceedings to satisfy the judgement against him. He was also black-listed with the studios and so it was sheer luck on his part that the maverick Howard Hughes took a chance on hiring him. It could well be that his long periods of inactivity in the Thirties were as a direct or indirect result of this studio disfavour, but that we shall never know.

He was never a studio workhorse, in the sense of a Michael Curtiz or a Woody Van Dyke, taking any project handed him. Even the later work for Fox in the Fifties shows a consistency in material which fell in line with the ideas that he was expressing in his films. And more than any other director, he was able to pursue his constant interest in a particular type of film throughout his career: *All Quiet on the Western Front* contains as many scenes of violence as any of his other war films; as Milestone himself said in an interview in "Action" (July-August, 1972): "How can you make a pacifist film without showing the violence of war?" The problem of making a classic film early in a career is that it sets a standard of comparison for all future work that is in some instances unfair. It should not be forgotten that Milestone also achieved his early reputation as a director of comedy, and he later worked on musicals, dramas, melodramas and a biography. His craftsmanship displayed itself as part of a whole; he employed many of the top technicians in the business to obtain his effects, co-ordinating their efforts and sublimating his personal role so that the direction seemed to be effortless: this surely is the skill of the true professional craftsman.

It should also be noted that *A Walk in the Sun* fell into the same category in England as Ford's *They Were Expendable* and Walsh's *Objective Burma,* that of a problem film. At the end of the war, it was felt that audiences were satiated with war movies, so Ford's film received a very limited showing; then Walsh's film caused a public protest on the grounds of bias and was withdrawn completely until the early Fifties. Milestone's film was not shown at all in Britain until 1951, by which time it had built up an overseas reputation which had an effect on its critical reception when it was eventually shown. One group of critics praised it for structure, poetic quality and technical mastery, while another group hated it on the grounds that it contained "too much talk and too little action," while both groups inevitably raised the comparison with *All Quiet on the Western Front.* Thus Milestone's experience with *Ocean's Eleven* was not the first time his career was affected by a poor decision on timing and distribution.

It is ironic and disturbing that the work of many of the Hollywood professionals like Milestone is only available to new generations of film audiences largely through the alternative medium of television, with the exception of certain famous films like *All Quiet on the Western Front* and *Of Mice and Men.* Television was thought to be the mortal enemy of the cinema, yet today it is serving film history at least by providing rare opportunities to see films by the old masters, albeit in an unsatisfactory form.

Gregory Peck and Rip Torn (centre) in PORK CHOP HILL

LEWIS MILESTONE Filmography

Miscellaneous:

THE FOOLISH AGE (1921, William Seiter). M. was an assistant director.

UP AND AT 'EM (1922, William Seiter). M. collaborated on the scenario.

MAIN STREET (1923, Harry Beaumont). M. was an assistant editor.

THE YANKEE CONSUL (1924, James W. Horne). M. collaborated on the story adaptation.

THE MAD WHIRL (1925, William Seiter). M. wrote the screen treatment.

DANGEROUS INNOCENCE (1925, William Seiter). M. wrote the story adaptation.

THE TEASER (1925, William Seiter). M. wrote the story adaptation.

BOBBED HAIR (1925, Alan Crosland Sr.). M. wrote the scenario.

FASCINATING YOUTH (1926, Sam Wood). M. played himself in a film studio sequence.

ALL QUIET ON THE WESTERN FRONT (1930, Lewis Milestone). M.'s hand appeared in the final shot.

THE GENERAL DIED AT DAWN (1936, Lewis Milestone). M. played a reporter.

Director:

SEVEN SINNERS (1925). Too many crooks spoil the haul, when they all rob the same mansion during a strike of Long Island private security guards. *Sc:* Lewis Milestone, Darryl F. Zanuck (from their story). *Ph:* David Abel. *Asst. ph:* Walter Robinson. *Asst. dir:* Frank Richardson. *With* Marie Prevost (*Molly Brian*), Clive Brook (*Jerry Winters*), John Patrick (*Handsome Joe Hagney*), Charles Conklin (*Scarlet Fever Sanders*), Claude Gillingwater (*Pious Joe McDowell*), Mathilde Brundage, Dan Mason, Fred Kelsey. *Prod:* Warner Bros. 7r.

THE CAVEMAN (1926). Social complications arise when a bored socialite introduces a coalman into society as an eccentric professor, and subsequently falls in love with him, only to find his skill as a ladykiller is unbeatable. *Sc:* Darryl F. Zanuck (from story "The Caveman" by Gelette Burgess). *Ph:* David Abel. *Asst. ph:* Frank Kesson. *Asst. dir:* D. Ross Lederman. *With* Matt Moore (*Mike Smagg*), Marie Prevost (*Myra Gaylord*), John Patrick (*Brewster Bradford*), Myrna Loy (*Maid*), Phyllis Haver (*Dolly Van Dream*), Hedda Hopper (*Mrs. Van Dream*). *Prod:* Warner Bros. 7r.

THE NEW KLONDIKE (1926). A baseball hero is dropped by a jealous coach, but makes a fortune by allowing his name to be used for real estate advertising. His team invest money with him, but lose all in a swindle; however all ends well as he recoups the money, earns the team managership and wins the girl. *Sc:* Thomas J. Geraghty (story by Ring Lardner). *Ph:* Alvin Wyckoff. *Art dir:* Walter E. Keller. *With* Thomas Meighan (*Tom Kelly*), Lila Lee (*Evelyn Lane*), Paul Kelly (*Bing Allen*), Hallie Manning (*Flamingo Applegate*), Robert Craig (*Morgan West*), George De Carlton; J. W. Johnston, Brenda Lane, Tefft

Johnson, Danny Hayes. Presented by Adolph Zukor, Jesse L. Lasky for Famous Players-Lasky. *Dist:* Paramount Pictures. 8r.

TWO ARABIAN KNIGHTS (1927). Two brawling soldiers escape from German captivity in the First World War by posing as Arabs on a ship bound for Jaffa. They fall for the same girl, upsetting local customs, but eventually manage to abscond successfully with her after defeating a band of cut-throats led by her father. *Sup:* John W. Considine Jnr. *Sc:* James T. O'Donohue, Wallace Smith (from story "Two Arabian Knights" by Donald McGibney). *Ph:* Antonio Gaudio, Joseph August. *Art dir:* William Cameron Menzies. *Titles:* George Marion Jnr. *Tech. dir:* Ned Mann. *Asst. dir:* Nate Watt. *With* William Boyd (*Pte. W. Dangerfield Phelps*), Mary Astor (*Anis Bin Adham/Mirza*), Louis Wolheim (*Sgt. Peter McGaffney*), Michael Vavitch (*Emir of Jaffa*), Ian Keith (*Shevket*), De Witt Jennings, Michael Visaroff, Boris Karloff. Presented by Howard Hughes, John W. Considine Jnr. for Caddo Company. *Dist:* United Artists. 9r.

THE GARDEN OF EDEN (1928). A comedy-drama with Corinne Griffith believing she has signed a contract to sing in opera, only to discover she has become a dance hall hostess. She loses the job, but becomes heir to a title and marries an eligible young man in spite of parental opposition to her past. *Sc:* Hans Kraly (from play "Der Garten Eden, Komödie in vier Akten" by Rudolf Bernauer, Rudolf Oesterreicher). *Ph:* John Arnold. *Set Design:* William Cameron Menzies. *Ed:* John Orlando.

Titles: George Marion Jnr. *With* Corinne Griffith (*Toni LeBrun*), Louise Dresser (*Rosa*), Lowell Sherman (*Henry von Glessing*), Maude George (*Madame Bauer*), Charles Ray (*Richard Spanyi*), Edward Martindel, Freeman Wood, Hank Mann. Presented by Walter Morosco. *Prod:* John W. Considine Jnr. for Feature Prods. *Dist:* United Artists. 8r.

THE RACKET (1928). A bootleg baron evades police authority with the backing of a powerful political boss until he kills a cop, and is hunted to the death by a vengeful police captain. *Sc:* Harry Behn, Del Andrews (a play by Bartlett Cormack). *Ph:* Tony Gaudio. *Ed:* Tom Miranda. *Titles:* Eddie Adams. *With* Thomas Meighan (*Captain McQuigg*), Marie Prevost (*Helen Hayes*), Louis Wolheim (*Nick Scarsi*), George Stone (*Joe Scarsi*), John Darrow (*Ames*), Skeets Gallagher, Lee Moran, Lucien Prival, Tony Marlo, Sam De Grasse, Burr McIntosh, G. Pat Collins. Presented by Howard Hughes for Caddo Company/Paramount Famous Lasky Corporation. 8r. Re-made by Hughes in 1951 with John Cromwell as director.

BETRAYAL (1929). Soap-opera about an artist leaving a village maid pregnant. Her father forces her to marry the mayor, and she refuses to take up with the artist on his return. She and the artist are involved in a fatal toboggan accident, and he claims paternity of one of her children. The mayor persecutes the boy but is eventually won over by love and reason. *Sc:* Hans Kraly (from story by Victor Schertzinger, Nicholas Saussanin). *Ph:* Henry Gerrard. *Art dir:* Hans Dreier. *Ed:* Del Andrews. *Song composer:* J. S. Zamecnik. *Titles:* Julian Johnson. *With* Emil Jannings (*Poldi Moser*), Esther Ralston (*Vroni Moser*), Gary Cooper (*Andre Frey*), Jada Weller (*Hans*), Douglas Haig (*Peter*), Bodil Rosing, Ann Brody, Paul Guertmann, Leone Lane. *Assoc. Prod:* David O. Selznick for Paramount Famous Lasky Corporation. 8r. Both a silent version and one with a musical score and sound effects were released.

NEW YORK NIGHTS (1929). A chorus girl leaves her alcoholic husband for a gangster who involves her in murder, and threatens to kill her ex-husband when she goes back to him, but the police catch the gangster, allowing the couple to start life anew. *Sc:* Jules Furthman (from play "Tin Pan Alley" by Hugh Stanislaus Strange). *Ph:* Ray June. *Ed:* Hal Kern. *Song composers:* Al Jolson, Ballard MacDonald, Dave Dreyer. *Sup:* John W. Considine Jnr. *With* Norma Talmadge (*Jill Deverne*), Gilbert Roland (*Fred Deverne*), John Wray (*Joe Prividi*), Lilyan Tashman (*Peggy*), Mary Doran (*Ruthie Day*), Roscoe Karns (*Johnny Dolan*). Presented by Joseph M. Schenck for United Artists. 9r.

ALL QUIET ON THE WESTERN FRONT (1930). Milestone's classic anti-war film recounting the collective and individual experiences of a group of raw recruits in the German Army. *Sc:* Maxwell Anderson, Del Andrews, George Abbott, Lewis Milestone (uncredited) (from novel by Erich Maria Remarque). *Dialogue:* Maxwell Anderson, George Abbott. *Dialogue dir:* George Cukor. *Ph:* Arthur Edeson, Karl Freund (final scene only), Tony Gaudio (2nd camera). *Special effects ph:* Frank H. Booth. *Art dir:* Charles D. Hall, William R. Schmidt. *Ed:* Edgar Adams, Milton Carruth. *Music and synchronisation:* David Broekman. *Asst. dir:* Nate Watt. *With* Lew Ayres (*Paul Baumer*), Louis Wolheim (*Katczinsky*), John Wray (*Himmelstross*), Raymond Griffith (*Gerard Duval*), George "Slim" Summerville (*Tjaden*), Russell Gleason, William Bakewell, Scott Kolk, Walter Browne Rogers, Ben Alexander, Owen Davis Jnr., Beryl Mercer, Edwin Maxwell, Harold Goodwin, Marion Clayton, G. Pat Collins, Richard Alexander, Yola D'Avril, Arnold Lacy, Bill Irving, Joan Marsh, Renee Damonde, Poupee Andriot, Edmund Breese, Heinie Conklin, Bertha Mann, Bodil Rosing, Tom London, Vincent Barnett, Fred Zinnemann. *Prod:* Carl Laemmle Jnr. for Universal. 140m. Current release version 107m.

THE FRONT PAGE (1931). A group of reporters awaiting the execution of a man convicted of killing a black policeman, do their utmost to make the event a front page story. *Sc:* Bartlett Cormack (from a play "The Front Page" by Ben Hecht, Charles MacArthur). *Dialogue:* Bartlett Cormack, Charles Lederer. *Ph:* Started by Tony Gaudio, finished by Hal Mohr, Glen McWilliams. *Art dir:* Richard Day. *Ed:* W. Duncan Mansfield. *With* Adolphe Menjou (*Walter Burns*), Pat O'Brien (*Hildy Johnson*), Mary Brian (*Peggy*), Edward Everett Horton (*Bensinger*), Walter Catlett (*Murphy*), George E. Stone, Mae Clarke, Slim Summerville, Matt Moore, Frank McHugh, Clarence H. Wilson, Fred Howard, Phil Tead, Eugene Strong, Spencer Charters, Maurice Black, Effie Ellsler, Dorothea Wolbert, James Gordon, Don Alexander. *Prod:* Howard Hughes for United Artists. 101m. Re-made as HIS GIRL FRIDAY (1940, *d* Howard Hawks).

RAIN (1932). A prostitute, stranded on Pago Pago, is pressured by fanatical missionaries to reform or else be deported. The hypocritical Reverend Davidson's lust overcomes him and he assaults her, later committing suicide, while Sadie ends up with a friendly sergeant. *Sc:* Maxwell Anderson (from a play by John Colton, Al Randolph and a story by Somerset Maugham). *Ph:* Oliver Marsh. *Art dir:* Richard Day. *Ed:* W. Duncan Mansfield. *With* Joan Crawford (*Sadie Thompson*), Walter Huston (*Reverend Davidson*), William Gargan (*Sgt. O'Hara*), Matt Moore (*Doctor MacPhail*), Beulah Bondi (*Mrs. Davidson*), Kendall Lee, Guy Kibbee, Walter Catlett, Ben Hendricks Jnr., Frederic Howard. *Prod:* for Allied Artists. 94m. Earlier version SADIE THOMPSON (1928, *d* Raoul Walsh); re-made as MISS SADIE THOMPSON (1953, *d* Curtis Bernhardt).

HALLELUJAH, I'M A BUM [GB: HALLELUJAH, I'M A TRAMP] (1933). An expression of the calm philosophy of a tramp, who temporarily reforms when he rescues and falls in love with an amnesiac girl. *Sc:* S. N. Behrman (from a story by Ben Hecht). *Musical Dialoguers:* Richard Rodgers, Laurenz Hart. *Ph:* Lucien Andriot. *Art dir:* Richard Day. *Music dir:* Alfred Newman. *With* Al Jolson (*Bumper*), Madge Evans (*June Marcher*), Harry Langdon (*Egghead*), Frank Morgan (*Mayor Hastings*), Chester Conklin (*Sunday*), Tyler Brooke,

Bert Roach, Edgar Conner, Dorothea Wolbert, Louise Carver, Tammany Young. *Prod:* for United Artists. 82m. Reissued in 1953 as LAZY BONES, running 63m. Alternative titles are NEW YORK, THE HEART OF NEW YORK, HAPPY GO LUCKY and THE OPTIMIST.

THE CAPTAIN HATES THE SEA (1934). Satirical commentary on pleasure cruises, with an underlying dramatic basis. *Sc:* Wallace Smith (from his story). *Ph:* Joseph August. *Ed:* Gene Milford. *With* Victor McLaglen (*Schulte*), John Gilbert (*Steve Bramley*), Walter Connolly (*Capt. Helquist*), Alison Skipworth (*Mrs. Magruder*), Wynne Gibson (*Mrs. Jeddock*), Helen Vinson (*Janet Grayson*), Fred Keating, Tala Birrell, Jerry Howard, Larry Fine, Moe Howard, Leon Errol, Walter Catlett, Claude Gillingwater, Emily Fitzroy, Geneva Mitchell, John Wray, Donald Meek, Luis Alberni, Akim Tamiroff, Arthur Treacher, Inez Courtney. *Prod:* for Columbia. 92m. (cut to 84m. in GB). Original length 103m.

PARIS IN SPRING [GB: PARIS LOVE SONG] (1935). A Parisian farce designed to boost the careers of the two leads; Carminati had just made a similar, highly successful film with Grace Moore, and Mary Ellis was being launched as Paramount's answer to Grace Moore. *Sc:* Samuel Hoffenstein, Franz Schulz, Keene Thompson (from play by Dwight Taylor). *Ph:* Ted Tetzlaff. *Art dir:* Hans Dreier, Ernst Fegte. *Ed:* Eda Warren. *Music:* Harry Revel. *With* Mary Ellis (*Simone*), Tullio Carminati (*Paul d'Orlando*), Ida Lupino (*Mignon de Charelle*), Lynne Overman

(*Dupont*), James Blakeley (*Albert de Charelle*), Jessie Ralph, Dorothy Wolbert, Akim Tamiroff, Harold Entwistle, Arnold Korff, Hugh Enfield, Joseph North, Rolfe Sedan, Arthur Houseman, Jack Raymond, Sam Ashe, Jack Mulhall. *Prod:* Benjamin Glazer for Paramount. 82m.

ANYTHING GOES (1936). Another shipboard comedy featuring Bing Crosby as a susceptible young man, who stows away on an ocean liner, in pursuit of his true love, but becomes a wanted man after falling in with crooks. *Sc:* Howard Lindsay, Russell Crouse, Guy Bolton, P. G. Wodehouse. *Ph:* Karl Struss. *Art dir:* Hans Dreier, Ernst Fegte. *Ed:* Eda Warren. *Music and lyrics:* Cole Porter. *Add. songs:* Leo Robin, Richard A. Whiting, Frederick Hollander, Hoagy Carmichael. *With* Bing Crosby (*Billy Crocker*), Ethel Merman (*Reno Sweeney*), Charles Ruggles (*Rev. Dr. Moon*), Ida Lupino (*Hope Harcourt*), Grace Bradley (*Bonnie Le Tour*), Arthur Treacher, Robert McWade, Richard Carle, Margaret Dumont, Jerry Tucker, Ed Gargan, Matt McHugh, Harry Wilson, Bud Fine, Billy Dooley, Matt Moore, Rolfe Sedan, Alan Ladd, Jack Mulhall, The Avalon Boys. *Prod:* Benjamin Glazer for Paramount. 92m. Retitled TOPS IS THE LIMIT for TV showings; title re-used for 1956 film starring Crosby, and directed by Robert Lewis.

THE GENERAL DIED AT DAWN (1936). An adventurer takes the side of oppressed Chinese peasants against a tyrannical war lord. *Sc:* Clifford Odets (from a novel by Charles G. Booth). *Ph:* Victor Milner. *Art dir:*

Hans Dreier, Ernst Fegte. *Ed:* Eda Warren. *Music:* Werner Janssen. *With* Gary Cooper (*O'Hara*), Madeleine Carroll (*Judy Perrie*), Akim Tamiroff (*General Yang*), Porter Hall (*Peter Perrie*), William Frawley (*Brighton*), Philip Ahn (*Oxford*), Lee Tung Foo, Leonid Kinskey, Val Duran, Willie Fung, Hans Furberg, Sarah Edwards, Paul Harvey, Spencer Chan, Harold Tong, Charles Leong, Thomas Chan, Harry Yip, Swan Yee, Kam Tong, Frank Young, Walter Wong, Carol De Castro, Barnett Parker, Hans von Morhart, Dudley Lee, Walter Lem, Thomas Lee, George Wong Wah, Tom Ung, Taft Jung, Sam Laborador, Richard Young, Jung Kai, George Chan, Clifford Odets, John O'Hara, Sidney Skolsky, Lewis Milestone. *Prod:* William Le Baron for Paramount. 95m.

OF MICE AND MEN (1939). John Steinbeck's literary classic of some of the less pleasant aspects of life in the Deep South involving a half-wit and his friend who become the subject of a manhunt. *Sc:* Eugene Solow (from a novel by John Steinbeck). *Ph:* Norbert Brodine. *Art dir:* Nicolai Remisoff. *Ed:* Bert Jordan. *Music:* Aaron Copland. *With* Burgess Meredith (*George*), Betty Field (*Mae*), Lon Chaney Jnr. (*Lennie*), Charles Bickford (*Slim*), Roman Bohnen (*Candy*), Bob Steele, Noah Beery Jnr., Granville Bates, Oscar O'Shea, Leigh Whipper. *Prod:* Lewis Milestone for Hal Roach. *Assoc. Prod:* Frank Ross. *Dist:* Hal Roach Studios/United Artists. 104m.

THE NIGHT OF NIGHTS (1939). A playwright ruins his career by appearing dead drunk at the first night of his play. His wife dies after leaving him, but many years later his daughter triumphs in a revival of the play, leaving him to die a contented man. *Sc:* Donald Ogden Stewart. *Ph:* Leo Tover. *Art dir:* Hans Dreier, ? *Ed:* Doane Harrison, Hugh Bennett. *With* Pat O'Brien (*Dan O'Farrell*), Olympe Bradna (*Alyce Farrell*), Roland Young (*Barry Trimble*), Reginald Gardiner (*Michael Fordin*), George E. Stone (*Sammy Kayn*), Murray Alper, Frank Sully, Russ Powell, Charles Miller, Pat O'Malley, Frank Shannon, Ronnie Rondell, Oscar O'Shea, Aileen Pringle, Laura Treadwell, A. L. Sherwood. *Prod:* George Arthur for Paramount. 86m.

LUCKY PARTNERS (1940). Comedy about an artist with a shady past, posing as a cartoonist, who wins a sweepstake draw with a girl, and talks her into going on a platonic honeymoon to Niagara Falls with ensuing complications involving her suspicious *fiancé* and the police. *Sc:* Allan Scott, John Van Druten (from a Sacha Guitry play "Bonne chance"). *Ph:* Robert de Grasse. *Art dir:* Van Nest Polglase. *Ed:* Henry Berman. *Music:* Dimitri Tiomkin. *With* Ronald Colman (*David*), Ginger Rogers (*Jean*), Jack Carson (*Freddie*), Spring Byington (*Aunt*), Cecilia Loftus (*Mrs. Sylvester*), Harry Davenport, Hugh O'Connell, Brandon Tynan, Leon Belasco, Edward Conrad, Walter Kingsford, Lucile Gleason, Helen Lynd. *Prod:* Harry E. Edington, George Haight for RKO. 102m.

MY LIFE WITH CAROLINE (1941). A frothy, disarming comedy, narrated in flashback by Ronald Colman, illustrating how he saved his wife from precipitate elopements with her sympathetic admirers. *Sc:* John Van Druten, Arnold Belgard (from a play "Train to Venice" by Louis Verneuil, Georges Berr). *Ph:* Victor Milner. *Prod. Design:* Nicolai Remisoff. *Ed:* Henry Berman. *Music:* Werner Heymann. *With* Ronald Colman (*Anthony*), Anna Lee (*Caroline*), Charles Winninger (*Bliss*), Reginald Gardiner (*Paul*), Gilbert Roland (*Paco Del Valle*), Katherine Leslie, Hugh O'Connell, Murray Alper, Matt Moore. *Prod:* Lewis Milestone. *Exec. Prod:* William Hawks for United Producers. *Dist:* RKO. 81m.

OUR RUSSIAN FRONT (1942). A documentary constructed from fifteen thousand feet of Russian newsreel footage. *Ed:* Lewis Milestone. *Commentary:* Elliot Paul. *Narrator:* Walter Huston. *Music:* Dimitri Tiomkin. *Co-prod:* Joris Ivens, Lewis Milestone.

EDGE OF DARKNESS (1943). An action-drama depicting Norwegian resistance against the Germans, ably scripted by Robert Rossen, one of Milestone's most interesting collaborators. *Sc:* Robert Rossen (from a story by William Woods). *Ph:* Sid Hickox. *Art dir:* Robert Haas. *Ed:* David Weisbart. *Music:* Franz Waxman. *With* Errol Flynn (*Gunnar Brogge*), Ann Sheridan (*Karen Stensgard*), Walter Huston (*Dr. Martin Stensgard*), Nancy Coleman (*Katja*), Judith Anderson (*Gerd Bjarnsen*), Helmut Dantine (*Capt. Koenig*), Tom Fadden, Ruth Gordon, Charles Dingle, John Beal, Roman Bohnen, Helen Thimig, Monte Blue, Dorothy Tree, Richard Fraser, Morris Carnovsky, Art Smith, Henry Brandon, Tonio Selwart, Torben Meyer, Frank Wilcox, Francis Pierlot, Lottie Williams, Virginia Christine, Henry Rowland. *Prod:* Henry Blanke for Warner Bros. *Exec. Prod:* Jack L. Warner. 120m.

THE NORTH STAR (1943). Another war drama, depicting the effects of German invasion on a small Russian village in the spring of 1940. Later re-issued as ARMORED ATTACK with additional footage changing the pro-Russian balance of the film. *Sc:* Lillian Hellman (from her own story). *Ph:* James Wong Howe. *Art dir:* Perry Ferguson. *Ed:* Daniel Mandell. *Music:* Aaron Copland. *With* Anne Baxter (*Marina*), Dana Andrews (*Kolya*), Walter Huston (*Dr. Kurin*), Walter Brennan (*Karp*), Ann Harding (*Sophia*), June Withers, Erich von Stroheim, Dean Jagger, Carl Benton Reid, Eric Roberts, Anne Carter, Esther Dale, Ruth Nelson, Paul Guilfoyle, Martin Kosleck, Tonio Selwart, Peter Pohlenz, Robert Lowery, Gene O'Donnell, Frank Wilcox, Loudie Claar, Lynn Winthrop, Charles Bates. *Prod:* Sam Goldwyn for RKO distribution. 105m.

THE PURPLE HEART (1944). The story of a show trial by the Japanese of the crew of an American Flying Fortress, shot down in action. *Sc:* Jerome Cady (from a story by Melville Crossman). *Ph:* Arthur Miller. *Art dir:* James Basevi, Lewis Creber. *Ed:* Douglas Biggs. *Music:* Alfred Newman. *With* Dana Andrews (*Capt. Ross*), Richard Conte (*Lt. Angelo Canelli*), Farley Granger (*Sgt. Howard Clinton*), Kevin O'Shea (*Sgt. Jan Skvoznik*), Donald Barry (*Lt. Peter Vincent*), Trudy Marshall, Sam Levene, Charles Russell, John Craven, Tala Birell, Richard Loo, Peter Chong, Gregory Gaye, Torben Meyer,

Kurt Katch, Martin Garralaga, Erwin Kaiser, Igor Dolgoruki, Nestor Paiva, Alex Papana, H. T. Tsiang, Benson Fong, Key Chang, Allen Jung, Wing Foo, Paul Fung, Joseph Kim, Luke Chan, Beal Wong, Marshall Thompson. *Prod:* Darryl F. Zanuck for 20th Century-Fox. 100m.

GUEST IN THE HOUSE (1944). A young girl taken into an average household starts poisoning family feeling. The lead role provided Anne Baxter with a good dress rehearsal for her part in Joseph L. Mankiewicz's ALL ABOUT EVE (1950). *Dir:* John Brahm [Andre de Toth and Lewis Milestone uncredited]. *Sc:* Ketti Frings (from a story by Hagar Wilde, Dale Eunson). *Ph:* Lee Garmes. *Prod. design:* Nicolai Remisoff. *Ed:* James Newcomb. *Music:* Werner Janssen. *With* Anne Baxter (*Evelyn Heath*), Ralph Bellamy (*Douglas Proctor*), Aline MacMahon (*Aunt Martha*), Ruth Warrick (*Ann Proctor*), Scott McKay (*Doctor Dan*), Jerome Cowan, Marie McDonald, Percy Kilbride, Margaret Hamilton, Connie Laird. *Prod:* Hunt Stromberg for United Artists. 121m.

A WALK IN THE SUN (1945). A literate and poetic account of men in war, concentrating on the experiences of an infantry platoon assigned to capture a German-occupied farmhouse in Italy. British release delayed until February 1951, after the anti-American furore created by Raoul Walsh's OBJECTIVE BURMA (1945). *Sc:* Robert Rossen (from a story by Harry Joe Brown). *Ph:* Russell Harlan. *Art dir:* Max Bertisch. *Ed:* W. Duncan Mansfield. *Music:* Frederic Efrem Rich. *With*

Dana Andrews (*Sgt. Tyne*), John Ireland (*Windy*), Richard Conte (*Riviera*), Sterling Holloway (*McWilliams*), George Tyne (*Friedman*), Herbert Rudley, Richard Benedict, Norman Lloyd, Lloyd Bridges, Huntz Hall, James Cardwell, Chris Drake, George Offerman Jnr., Alvin Hammer, Steve Brodie, Norman Willis, Robert Lowell, Anthony Dante, Robert Horton, John Kellogg, Jay Norris. *Prod:* Lewis Milestone for 20th Century-Fox. 117m.

THE STRANGE LOVE OF MARTHA IVERS (1946). A childhood skeleton surfaces, threatening to destroy the career of a rising politician, when his faithless wife tries to manipulate an old friend who has drifted back into town. *Sc:* Robert Rossen (from a story by John Patrick). *Ph:* Victor Milner. *Art dir:* Hans Dreier, John Meehan. *Ed:* Archie Marshek. *Music:* Miklos Rozsa. *With* Barbara Stanwyck (*Martha Ivers*), Van Heflin (*Sam Masterton*), Kirk Douglas (*Walter O'Neil*), Lizabeth Scott (*Toni Maracek*), Judith Anderson (*Mrs. Ivers*), Darryl Hickman, Janis Wilson, Mickey Kuhn, Frank Orth, Roman Bohnen, Ann Doran, James Flavin, Charles D. Brown, John Kellogg, Tommy Ryan, Don Fadden. *Prod:* Hal B. Wallis for Paramount. 116m.

ARCH OF TRIUMPH (1948). A refugee doctor falls in love with a girl with a past in Paris just prior to the Nazi invasion of France. *Sc:* Lewis Milestone, Harry Joe Brown (from a novel by Erich Maria Remarque). *Ph:* Russell Harlan. *Prod. design:* William Cameron Menzies. *Ed:* W. Duncan Mansfield. *Music:* Morris Stoloff. *With* Charles Boyer (*Ravic*), Ingrid Bergman (*Joan Madou*), Charles Laughton (*Haake*), Louis Calhern (*Morosow*), Roman Bohnen (*Dr. Veber*), Ruth Warrick, Stephen Bekassy, Ruth Nelson, Curt Bois, J. Edward Bromberg, Michael Romanoff, Art Smith, John Laurenz, Leon Lenoir, Franco Corsaro, Nino Pipitoni, Vladimir Rashevsky, Alvin Hammer, Jay Gilpin, Ella Tamara, Andre Marsauden, Hazel Brooks, Byron Foulger, William Conrad, Peter Virgo, Feodor Chaliapin. *Prod:* David Lewis for United Artists. 120m. Ruth Warrick's role was largely eliminated due to drastic re-editing; the British running time was 114m.

NO MINOR VICES (1948). A doctor brings home an eccentric artist, who falls in love with April, the doctor's wife, creating such havoc at home and in the clinic that the doctor's marriage and career are nearly destroyed. *Sc:* Arnold Manoff (from his own story). *Ph:* George Barnes. *Art dir:* Nicolai Remisoff. *Ed:* Robert Parrish. *Music:* Franz Waxman. *With* Dana Andrews (*Dr. Perry Aswill*), Lilli Palmer (*April*), Louis Jourdan (*Octavio Quaglini*), Jane Wyatt (*Miss Darlington*), Norman Lloyd (*Dr. Sturdivant*), Bernard Gorcey, Roy Roberts, Fay Baker, Sharon McManus, Ann Doran, Beau Bridges, Frank Kreig, Kay Williams, Bobby Hyatt. *Prod:* Lewis Milestone for Enterprise. *Dist:* M-G-M. 96m.

THE RED PONY (1949). An adaptation of a John Steinbeck story about a ranchboy who is given a gift of a colt, whom he comes to love, but then the colt escapes to freedom. *Sc:* John Steinbeck (from his own story). *Ph:* Tony Gaudio. *Prod. design:* Nicolai

Richard Widmark with Reginald Gardiner and Jack Webb in
HALLS OF MONTEZUMA

Remisoff. *Art dir:* Victor Greene. *Ed:* Harry Keller. *Music:* Aaron Copland. *With* Myrna Loy (*Alice Tiflin*), Robert Mitchum (*Billy Buck*), Louis Calhern (*Grandfather*), Shepperd Strudwick (*Fred Tiflin*), Peter Miles (*Tom*), Margaret Hamilton, Patty King, Jackie Jackson, Beau Bridges, Little Brown Jug, Nino Temp, Tommy Sheridan. *Prod:* Lewis Milestone for Republic. Technicolor. 89m.

HALLS OF MONTEZUMA (1951). Action drama depicting the American Marines taking on the Japanese, as well as their own fears and problems with some help from the British in the person of Reginald Gardiner. *Sc:* Michael Blankfort (from his own story). *Ph:* Winton C. Hoch, Harry Jackson. *Art dir:* Lyle Wheeler, Albert Hogstett. *Ed:* William Reynolds. *Music:* Sol Kaplan. *With* Richard Widmark (*Anderson*), Walter Jack Palance (*Pigeon Lane*), Reginald Gardiner (*Johnson*), Robert Wagner (*Coffman*), Karl Malden (*Doc*), Richard Boone, Richard Hylton, Skip Homeier, Don Hicks, Jack Webb, Bert Freed, Neville Brand, Martin Milner, Philip Ahn, Howard Chuman, Frank Kumagai, Fred Coby, Paul Lees, Jack

115

Finlay Currie in KANGAROO

Lee, Fred Dale, Chris Drake, George Conrad, Harry McKim, Bob McLean, William Hawes, Roger McGee, Clarke Stevens, Helen Hatch, Michael Road. *Prod:* Robert Bassler for 20th Century-Fox. Technicolor. 113m.

KANGAROO (1952). A drama casting Peter Lawford as a sailor who becomes involved in a mysterious case of mistaken identity. *Sc:* Harry Kleiner (from a story by Martin Berkeley). *Ph:* Charles G. Clarke. *Art dir:* Lyle Wheeler, Mark Lee-Kirk. *Ed:* Nick De Maggio. *Music:* Sol Kaplan. *With* Peter Lawford (*Richard Connor*), Maureen O'Hara (*Dell McGuire*), Finlay Currie (*Michael McGuire*), Richard Boone (*Gamble*), Chips Rafferty (*Trooper Leonard*), Lefty Craydon, Charles Tingwell, Ron Whelan, John Fegan, Guy Doleman, Reg Collins, Frank Ransom, Clyde Combo, Henry Murdoch. *Prod:* Robert Bassler for 20th Century-Fox. Technicolor. 84m.

LES MISERABLES (1952). Adaptation of Victor Hugo's classic novel about a man who is imprisoned for stealing a loaf of bread, and then hounded by the arresting officer, who trails him for a lifetime. *Sc:* Richard Murphy (from a novel by Victor Hugo). *Ph:* Joseph La Schelle. *Art dir:* Lyle Wheeler, J. Russell Spencer. *Sets:* Thomas Little, Walter M. Scott. *Ed:* Hugh Fowler. *Music:* Alec North. *With* Michael Rennie (*Jean Valjean*), Debra Paget (*Cosette*), Robert Newton (*Javert*), Edmund Gwenn (*Bishop*), Sylvia Sidney (*Fantine*), Cameron Mitchell, Elsa Lanchester, James Robertson Justice, Joseph Wiseman, Rhys Williams, Florence Bates, Merry Anders, John Rogers,

Robert Newton and Debra Paget in LES MISERABLES

Charles Keane, John Dierkes, John Costello, Norma Varden, William Cottrell, Queenie Leonard, Bobby Hyatt, Sanders Clark, Sean McClory, Jean Vachon, Guy Miali, John O'Malley, Jack Reitzen, Leslie Denison, John Dodsworth, Alex Frazer, June Hillman, Jack Raine, James Craven, John Sherman, Dayton Lummis, Lester Matthews, Jimmie Moss, Ian Wolfe, Victor Wood, Herbert Deans, Alfred Linder. *Prod:* Fred Kohlmar for 20th Century-Fox. 104m. Previous American version filmed in 1935 by Richard Boleslawski.

MELBA (1953). Biography of the opera star, Dame Nellie Melba. *Sc:* Harry Kurnitz (from his own story). *Ph:* Ted Scaife [and Arthur Ibbetson]. *Art dir:* Andre Andrejev. *Ed:* William J. Lewthwaite. *Music:* Muir Mathieson. *With* Patricia Munsel (*Nellie Melba*), Robert Morley (*Oscar Hammerstein*), John McCallum (*Charles Armstrong*), John Justin (*Eric Walton*), Alec Clunes (*Cesar Carlton*), Martita Hunt, Dame Sybil Thorndyke, Joseph Tomelty, Beatrice Varley, Violetta Elvin. *Prod:* S. P. Eagle [Sam Spiegel] for Horizon. *Dist:* United Artists. Technicolor. 112m.

THEY WHO DARE (1953). A team of British and Greek soldiers is assigned to destroy airfields in Rhodes when Allied communication lines are being hampered by the Germans. *Sc:* Robert Westerby. *Ph:* Wilkie Cooper. *Art dir:* Don Ashton. *Ed:* V. Sagovsky. *Music:* Robert Gill. *With* Dirk Bogarde (*Lieut. Graham*), Denholm Elliott (*Sgt. Corcoran*), Akim Tamiroff (*Capt. George One*), Gerard Oury (*Capt. George Two*), Eric Pohlmann (*Capt. Papadopoulos*), Alec Mango, Kay Callard,

Russell Enoch (later William Russell), Sam Kydd, Peter Burton, David Peel, Michael Mellinger, Lisa Gastoni, Harold Siddons, Anthea Leigh, Eileen Way. *Prod:* Aubrey Baring, Maxwell Setton for Mayflower Pictures. *Dist:* British Lion. Technicolor. 107m.

LA VEDOVA (GB: THE WIDOW) (1955). A high-powered romantic melodrama, filmed in Italy with an international cast. *Sc:* Louis Stevens (from a novel by Susan York). *Adapt:* Lewis Milestone. *Ph:* Arturo Gallea. *Music:* Mario Nascimbene. *With* Patricia Roc (*Diana*), Anna Maria Ferrero (*Adriana*), Massimo Serato (*Vittorio*), Akim Tamiroff (*The Uncle*), Leonard Botta (*Bonelli*). *Prod:* John G. Nasht for Venturini/Express. 90m (cut to 81 for British release).

PORK CHOP HILL (1959). The story of a battle for a strategic point of little military value, but of great moral value, during the last days of the Korean War. *Dir:* Lewis Milestone. *Sc:* James R. Webb (from a story by S. L. A. Marshall, U.S.A.R.). *Ph:* Sam Leavitt. *Prod. design:* Nicolai Remisoff. *Ed:* George Boemler. *Music:* Leonard Roseman. *With* Gregory Peck (*Lieut. Joe Clemons*), Harry Guardino (*Forstman*), George Shibata (*Lieut. Tsugi O'Hashi*), Woody Strode (*Franklin*), James Edwards (*Cpl. Jurgens*), Rip Torn, George Peppard, Bob Steele, Norman Fell, Robert Blake, Biff Elliott, Barry Atwater, Michael Garth, Ken Lynch, Paul Comi, Abel Fernandez, Lou Gallo, Cliff Ketchum, Bert Remson, Martin Landau, Kevin Hagen, Dean Stanton, Leonard Graves, Syl Lamont, Gavin McCloud, John Alderman, John McKee, Charles Aidman, Chuck Hayward, Buzz Martin, Robert Williams, William Wellman Jnr., Viraj Amonsin, Barry McGuire and Carl Benton Reid. *Prod:* Sy Bartlett for Melville. *Dist:* United Artists. 97m.

OCEAN'S ELEVEN (1960). A comedy about a gang who are brought together to heist a casino. *Sc:* Harry Brown, Charles Lederer (from a story by George Clayton Johnson, Jack Golden Russell). *Ph:* William H. Daniels. *Art dir:* Nicolai Remisoff. *Ed:* Philip W. Anderson. *Music:* Nelson Riddle. *With* Frank Sinatra (*Danny Ocean*), Dean Martin (*Sam Harmon*), Sammy Davis Jnr. (*Josh Howard*), Peter Lawford (*Jimmy Foster*), Angie Dickinson (*Beatrice Ocean*), Richard Conte (*Anthony Bergdorf*), Cesar Romero, Patrice Wymore, Joey Bishop, Akim Tamiroff, Henry Silva, Ilka Chase, Buddy Lester, Richard Benedict, Jean Willes, Norman Fell, Clem Harvey, Hank Henry, Red Skelton (guest), Shirley MacLaine (guest), George Raft (guest). *Prod:* Lewis Milestone for Dorchester. *Dist:* Warner Bros. *Assoc. Prod:* Henry W. Sanicola, Milton Ebbins. Technicolor, Panavision. 127m.

MUTINY ON THE BOUNTY (1962). A re-make of the Nordhoff-Hall saga about Fletcher Christian's opposition to the tyranny of Captain Bligh. *Dir:* Lewis Milestone (replacing Carol Reed—scenes also reputedly shot by Andrew Marton, George Seaton, Richard Thorpe, Billy Wilder and Fred Zinnemann). *Sc:* Charles Lederer (from a novel by Charles Nordhoff, James Norman Hall). *Ph:* Robert L. Surtees. *Art dir:* George W. Davis, J. McMillan Johnson. *Ed:* John McSweeney Jnr. *Music:* Bronislau Kaper. *With* Marlon Brando (*Fletcher Christian*), Trevor Howard (*Captain William Bligh*), Richard Harris (*John Mills*), Hugh Griffith (*Alexander Smith*), Richard Haydn (*William Brown*), Tim Seely, Percy Herbert, Gordon Jackson, Noel Purcell, Duncan Lamont, Chips Rafferty, Ashley Cowan, Eddie Byrne, Keith McConnell, Frank Silvera, Ben Wright, Torin Thatcher, Matahiarii Tama, Tarita. *Prod:* Aaron Rosenberg for Arcola. *Dist:* M-G-M. Technicolor, Ultra Panavision 70. 179m (cut from 185m). Re-make of 1935 film directed by Frank Lloyd.

Unrealised projects:

THINGS TO COME (1934). Negotiations with Alexander Korda fell through, and the film was finally made in Britain in 1936 with William Cameron Menzies directing.

DEAD END (1937). Sam Goldwyn hired Milestone and Clifford Odets to write a screenplay from Sidney Kingsley's play, but none of their work appeared in William Wyler's film.

ROAD SHOW (1938). Milestone worked on a screenplay, but had no connection with the 1940 film, directed by Hal Roach.

MOBY DICK (1943). This was announced as an Errol Flynn vehicle to be directed by Milestone; filmed in 1956 by John Huston.

KING KELLY (1957). Milestone worked on the project with Kirk Douglas about a "Kane" type tycoon for a year, but it was shelved.

P.T. 109 (1963). Milestone began

shooting the story of John F. Kennedy's war experiences, but was replaced by Leslie H. Martinson, and received no credit.

LA GUERRA SECRETA (1965). Milestone began an episode, but was replaced by Terence Young. Released in America as THE DIRTY GAME (1966), with other episodes directed by Christian-Jaque and Carlo Lizzani.

HALLS OF MONTEZUMA: Milestone's familiar man at war

Sam Wood on location with FOR WHOM THE BELL TOLLS

Sam Wood: A Master of His Craft

There was no identifiable personal style to mark Sam Wood's thirty years as a director in Hollywood. What can be said about Wood might also be said about a number of other highly competent directors in the heyday of the major studios: they thoroughly understood the business of making filmed entertainment. In the case of Sam Wood his track record was almost without blemish; he was dedicated to his life as a film-maker and he never lost his fascination for his work. His twenty years as a director under contract to Paramount and M-G-M built him the most solid of reputations, and he was able to enjoy the last ten years of his life as a free-lancer.

Sam Wood's career divides itself into two plateaux, equal in length but vastly different in quality. From 1920 to 1935 he directed fifty films and they were all ephemeral product. Then he was assigned, apparently with some persuasion, to direct the Marx Brothers in *A Night at the Opera* and the success of that classic eased Wood into another league. He went on to direct twenty-five other films and a half-dozen of them are films of which any director could be proud: *Goodbye, Mr. Chips, Our Town, Kings Row, The Pride of the Yankees, For Whom the Bell Tolls*, and *Ivy*. Again, there was no common denominator of style; Wood moved from the lightest of comedies to the darkest of dramas with ease. It was no Midas touch but it was assuredly the work of a thorough professional with a clear and vital mind.

Veteran Hollywood producer Sol Lesser, who first hired Wood in 1921 and for whom Wood directed the esteemed *Our Town*, remembers him as a man devoid of flamboyance: "I never knew Sam to socialise or carouse or behave in an artificial way. In that sense he was rather odd for those days. His manners and his dress were very conservative. He seemed to be like a gentlemanly business executive. In fact, he was very businesslike. Sam was quiet and gentle with people—but firm. He was also cost conscious, which was also unusual for those days, and he was one of the most conscientious men I've ever known in this business."

There seem to have been few complications in the life of Sam Wood, other than the extreme right-wing, vehemently anti-Communist political sentiments that became obsessive in his last years and, in the view of some, marred his image. His politics are perhaps understandable in the light of his background and his experience. Wood was an enterprising young man in the early years of the Twentieth century, at a time when the Horatio Alger concept of the American Dream was viable and workable. He had the luck to be in the right place at the right time and the vitality to pursue and develop his luck. It was Wood's good fortune not to need help from anyone.

Samuel Grosvenor Wood was born in Philadelphia on July 10, 1883, the son of a textile manufacturer. He was a bright but not brilliant student with a marked appetite for sports and athletics. Wood enjoyed football, swimming, and rowing in his young years, and in his maturity he was addicted to tennis, golf and general physical fitness. Many of his films touched upon his fondness for the athletic life, notably *The Pride of the Yankees* and *The Stratton Story*. His death from a heart attack at the age of sixty-five made his dedication to leading an active life seem somewhat ironic.

In the summer of 1901 Wood and a companion took off on a trip across the United States, destined for California but determined to adventure along the way. After a year of hitch-hiking and odd-jobbing Wood found himself in Los Angeles. He decided to stay and he looked around for an occupation. At this point he had no interest in the film industry. Real estate was flourishing in these early years of southern California being discovered as a comfortable place to live and Wood considered this a good business opportunity. By 1906, aged twenty-three, Sam Wood was well established as a real estate broker but it was in that year that a film company hired one of his properties as a location. Watching the company work Wood had the notion that this would be a good business to get into, mostly because he was not impressed with the way this particular film was being made, and felt he could easily do better.

Wood believed he could best learn about the film business by entering it as an actor and playing the role of an observer. He assumed the name Chad Applegate and played in a number of cheaply shot two-reelers. In these years of picture-making in California it was a business held in little repute and the clients of real estate broker Wood were unaware that he was also acting on the side. In 1908 Wood married Clara Louise Roush, who would be his wife until he died forty-one years later, and she encouraged him to take the film business seriously. In 1910 he was compelled to take films seriously when a real estate depression closed his business. Having no real interest in acting, Wood sought and found work as a production assistant. Four years later he graduated to the rank of assistant director and for two years worked for Cecil B. DeMille.

Sam Wood never kept a log of his activities but he calculated that he worked on several hundred pictures as an assistant director, most of them short, quickly made pictures. In late 1919, having been in the employ of Paramount for three years, Wood was finally given the opportunity he had been striving for—to direct. His first assignment was *Double Speed,* starring Wallace Reid, the success of which won him the direction of Reid's next four films. The Reid films were mostly fast-paced action comedies, running approximately one hour. The handsome, charming Reid was then at the peak of his considerable popularity and Wood's ability to

Bebe Daniels and Wallace Reid in THE DANCIN' FOOL

handle the assignments quickly established him as a director. All five of Wood's Reid pictures were released in 1920, as were three other Wood-directed films. It was a frantic first year as a director, unmatched in product output by any other year in his career.

In *Double Speed* Wallace Reid appeared as an auto racer named Speed Carr, who embarks on a marathon race from New York to Los Angeles and wins it after many adventures, including the loss of his car—he ends up driving a truck. The film was eagerly received by Reid's many fans, who had been won over by his breezy, dashing "racer" image in previous films. Paramount im-

Wood (left) with Gloria Swanson and Albert Gilks, the man who photographed all ten of the Wood-Swanson pictures

mediately lined up another vehicle for Wood: *Excuse My Dust*. They followed it with two non-racing pictures: *The Dancin' Fool*, and *Sick Abed*. Reid's leading lady in both pictures was nineteen-year-old Bebe Daniels, who had already spent most of her young years on the stage. As *The Dancin' Fool* the energetic Reid played a store clerk with hopes of becoming a famous dancer, which is what happened to him when he met up with dancer Bebe. Wood allowed the film to become serious in spots, thereby playing against the material and giving the silly script a little pathos. In

Sick Abed Reid was a rich young hypochondriac, finally cured of all his ailments by pretty but practical nurse Bebe. This film probably displeased the Reid idolators and Paramount immediately put him back behind a steering wheel for *What's Your Hurry?* This time he was not a cheeky racer but a valiant truck driver, leading a team of lumbering vehicles over muddy roads through the rain to deliver emergency supplies to a crew on a dam in danger of breaking. The critic in the "New York Times" noted: "In picturing the progress of the trucks, the struggles at the dam and the contrasting (Christmas) festivity in the endangered houses, and in assembling his scenes, Mr. Wood has displayed noteworthy cinematographic skill."

Jesse Lasky, then head of production at Paramount, later admitted: "We virtually turned these road-racing items out on an assembly line, and every one was a money maker." However, Paramount's luck with Wallace Reid was soon to break. Reid had been injured in a train mishap while on a film location in 1919 and in order not to hold up production he had been given morphine to ease his pain. He was thereafter afflicted with headaches and sciatica, and continued taking morphine, eventually becoming an addict. Reid, who was not only good box-office but greatly liked by his co-workers, died from his addiction in January 1923. The following April he would have been thirty-two. Reid was taking morphine during his films with Sam Wood but it had not presented a problem. However, after five films Wood asked to be assigned to other projects, despite Paramount's wish that he do more Reid vehicles. Perhaps as a sign of displeasure, the studio sent him to their subsidiary company, Realart, to do a series of routine programme pictures. The first was *A City Sparrow*, starring Ethel Clayton as a country girl who goes to the city to become an actress and who, after her success, returns to the country to find real happiness as a farm wife. This was followed by three films starring the pretty but vapid Wanda Hawley: *Her Beloved Villain*, *Her First Elopement*, and *The Snob*. The plots for these five-reelers could only have been a challenge to Wood in terms of their slightness; *The Snob*, for example, tells of a snobbish young lady who rejects her college boy friend when she learns he is working his way through college as a waiter. All her friends then conspire to get jobs as waiters in order to teach her a lesson. Miss Hawley's career in films did not last long but Wood survived his assignment to Realart.

Douglas Fairbanks Sr., Sam Wood, Rudolph Valentino, Elinor Glyn and Mary Pickford

Wood's output for 1920 left no doubt about his capability. Clearly here was an ideal director of film product—fast, efficient, able to command respect from his casts and crews, and with a flair for telling stories in a straightforward manner. Late that year Wood was given an opportunity which would advance his career rapidly. Paramount decided to make a star of Gloria Swanson and they asked Wood to direct her first starring vehicle, *The Great Moment*. Swanson had been in films for five years by this time; in 1919 she was contracted by Paramount and came under the influence of Cecil B. DeMille, who used her in five of his films, one after the other. It is possible that DeMille had much to do with Wood's being assigned to Swanson, and it is also possible that Swanson herself had a considerable say in the matter. She and Wood had become good friends; when the second of Wood's two daughters was born he named the child Gloria.

The Great Moment was the first of ten Swanson-Wood pictures. The popular novelist Elinor Glyn supplied the soap opera-like story, that of a fine English girl who runs off with a virile American engineer, played by the virile Milton Sills, and gets lost with him out West. They are eventually found by her distraught father, who forces the couple to marry. At one point in the film Swanson was bitten on the chest by a rattlesnake, causing Sills to suck the venom from her in order to save her life. This well calculated piece of sensationalism paid off handsomely. The shrewdly concocted scene was criticised in some quarters, leaving Milton Sills in his interviews with the press to explain that it was the only thing a man could have done under the circumstances.

Paramount awaited public reaction to *The Great Moment* before giving Wood another assignment. In between the completion of the film and its release, they allowed Wood to accept an offer from independent producer Sol Lesser to direct his *Peck's Bad Boy*, starring Jackie Coogan. Coogan had made a big impact on the public playing opposite Charlie Chaplin in *The Kid*, and Lesser quickly sought a starring vehicle for the seven-year old lad. The George Wilbur stories about Peck's mischievous son seemed like perfect source material for Coogan and Wood himself adapted the stories into a screenplay. The end result was not highly regarded by critics but it did no harm to Coogan, who went on to become the most popular movie youngster of silent films.

★   ★   ★

Swanson followed *The Great Moment* with a film for Cecil B. DeMille, *The Affairs of Anatol,* and then launched into a series of nine pictures with Sam Wood as her director. The films were made over a two-year period and employed much the same staff and crew. The same photographer was used on every one of them— Albert Gilks.

In *Under the Lash* Swanson played a drab young wife of a stern old Boer farmer, a man who ruled by the whip. Life was opened up and brightened for her by the appearance of an educated young Englishman, who also saved her from being killed by her husband. Next came a change of pace with *Don't Tell Everything*, a light comedy about two women competing for the same man. The man was played by Wallace Reid, in one of his last screen appearances. *Her Husband's Trademark* was another outlandish soap opera, of a kind for which there appears to have been a strong market in the early Twenties. Here Swanson was the wife of a vicious businessman who used her as a decoy and a dupe. He got his just deserts when he used her in a business deal involving an old boy-friend of hers.

Paramount was well pleased with the results of the Swanson-Wood pictures. The team worked smoothly and Swanson's popularity climbed with each film. Aiming for even higher results

Paramount called in Elinor Glyn to supply another glossy story, one in which they could co-star Swanson with Rudolph Valentino. Glyn came up with *Beyond the Rocks,* an improbable fable about the young wife of an elderly but understanding millionaire who disposes of himself so that she will be free to love the handsome chap of her choice. The film allowed for dream sequences in which Swanson and Valentino besported themselves in a variety of period costumes. The public appetite was whetted for more of the same. In *Her Gilded Cage* Swanson was a French actress who visits America and falls for a robust young artist, even though her name is romantically linked with a European monarch. As *The Impossible Mrs. Bellew,* Swanson suffered as the faithful wife of a brutal husband, who forced her into divorce on a trumped up charge of adultery. Mrs. Bellew then went to France to try and lead a life of gay abandon but gave it up when the right man came along.

The Swanson-Wood pictures continued in high gear. *My American Wife* co-starred her with Antonio Moreno, he as a dashing Latin American and she as a rich lass from the U.S.A. Together they survive the attacks of Argentinian bandits and settle down to happiness on the pampas. *Prodigal Daughters,* made in 1923, was thoroughly contemporary—a revel of the Roaring Twenties, with Gloria Swanson as a flapper called Swiftie. This was Hollywood's idea of New York society living it up; jazz, dancing, smoking, drinking and wearing daring modern clothes.

For their final film together Wood and Swanson decided on *Bluebeard's Eighth Wife,* which had been a hit play in New York with Ina Claire. In this Swanson played a French girl who learned on the eve of her marriage that her beloved had dumped his seven previous brides. She nonetheless proceeded with the marriage, convinced of her ability to become and remain the only woman in his life. This happy trifle completed the working association between the star and the director. All the films had been profitable but after ten of them both Swanson and Wood deemed it advisable to call a halt. Swanson's career continued on a high plane all through the remaining years of the Silent Era, and Wood had no trouble getting other assignments from Paramount, although there were signs of discontent in the Front Office over his tendency to argue with their choice of projects.

Wood's last 1923 release was *His Children's Children,* a rather heavy-handed morality tale. It told of a wealthy old man whose offspring were afflicted with avarice. Toward the end of the picture, as he lay dying in his bed, his grandchildren were downstairs auctioning off his possessions. The poor old fellow summoned enough strength to get up but he dropped dead when he saw what was going on. In his last grasp he dragged from the wall a plaque with the legend: "Except the Lord build the house, they labour in vain that build it." The sentiment would seem to have been ignored by the fun loving folk of the period.

Sam Wood balked at his next assignment, *Bluff,* starring Agnes Ayres. He felt Miss Ayres had no screen value and that Paramount was wasting its time grooming her for stardom. She had won some popularity playing opposite Valentino in *The Sheik* but Wood felt that she lacked sufficient magnetism to carry a film. *Bluff* turned out to be a tepid picture, which might have had something to do with Wood's own lack of enthusiasm. In it, Ayres played an unsuccessful model who posed as a missing celebrity whom she happened to resemble, not knowing that the celebrity had absconded with charity funds.

The Female was Wood's most unusual film of these years. It featured Betty Compson as the young bride of a rough old Boer, played by Noah Beery, and it gave some insight into life on the Veldt. The plot hinged on the pact the old man makes with his bride that she can do anything she likes for three years, after which she must settle down with him. Wood next accepted another offer from Sol Lesser, this time to direct a film for his newly formed Principal Pictures. It was Wood's first western although it was not of the regular variety: *The Mine with the Iron Door* told the story of a young girl, first kidnapped and then lost in the desert, who grows to womanhood with mining prospectors as her guardians. She falls in love with a young man accused of embezzlement, but he finally clears his name when he nails the real villains and the young couple find happiness, aided by the discovery of a gold mine. The girl was played by Dorothy Mackaill; she had also played in *His Children's Children* and she was the star of Wood's next picture for Paramount, *The Next Corner*. Here she played a woman torn between her love for her husband (Conway Tearle) and her infatuation with a handsome Spaniard (Ricardo Cortez). The picture was decked out with expensive production values—lavish parties in Paris and a spectacular storm in the mountains—but nothing could disguise its meagre plot.

By mid-1924 Sam Wood was a discontented director. He had not been happy with his last two Paramount assignments and now they asked him to direct another Agnes Ayres vehicle despite his previous contentions. Wood refused the project and when all discussions failed Paramount suspended him. Suspension of a contract director by a major studio in those days was tantamount to black listing but Wood was adamant in his stand. The consequence was a year of unemployment. Sol Lesser came to his rescue and offered him *The Recreation of Brian Kent,* a filming of a popular novel by Harold Bell Wright. More soap opera but this time from the male point of view; poor Brian Kent was a bank clerk forced to embezzle large sums to support a demanding wife. He

Opposite: "Red" Grange with Sam Wood and Mary McAllister while making ONE MINUTE TO PLAY

is saved from suicide by a young woman, whose love reforms him. Fortunately for the lovers the wife drowns. The film was money in the bank for Lesser and proof for Paramount that Wood was too good a director to let linger. They invited him home and gave him a lavish production, *Fascinating Youth*, a vehicle for sixteen prize graduates of the Paramount Talent School. Charles (Buddy) Rogers headed the cast and only he attained any measure of stardom. The light comedy included much doing of the Charleston and a lot of winter sports, but the picture was fleeting entertainment and it did nothing to convince Wood that he had any future with Paramount. He asked for, and got, a release from his contract.

Sam Wood was immediately hired by a small company called Robertson-Cole, managed by a Bostonian who would later enter politics, Joseph P. Kennedy. Robertson-Cole later changed its name to F.B.O. (Film Booking Office) and later still amalgamated with other interests to become RKO Radio Studios. Robertson-Cole had contracted the hottest football player of the day, Harold "Red" Grange, and convinced he would be equally hot at the movie box-office they asked Wood to direct him in *One Minute to Play*. As a football buff himself, Wood was able to inject the college football story with much vim and verve. "New York Times" critic Mordaunt Hall commented: "Wood uses his cameras effectively in the tense periods and his direction of the players is sound and sensible."

Nineteen twenty-seven was a good year for Sam Wood. It was a major turning point in his career. M-G-M asked him to direct two pictures for them, the success of which resulted in him gaining a long term contract with what was then, and would be for many years, Hollywood foremost studio. *Rookies* was a broad comedy concerning the antics of a Marine Corps drill sergeant (Karl Dane) and a song-and-dance man (George K. Arthur) drafted into service. The conflict between the two men provided the slapstick humour.

Wood followed this with a Marion Davies vehicle, *The Fair Co-Ed,* filmed mostly at Pomona College, near Los Angeles, and again allowing him to indulge his flair for depicting youthful athletic exuberance on the campus.

Robertson-Cole asked Wood to direct Harold "Red" Grange in another sports epic. *A Racing Romeo,* which must have struck Wood as a reminder of his days with Wallace Reid. Grange proved a poor bet as a film star and Wood wisely enlivened the picture with plenty of racetrack footage. By the time he had finished the Grange picture, his two M-G-M films had proven their market value and Wood then accepted a long term contract with that studio. All but one of his films over the next eleven years were M-G-M productions. He began 1928 by directing the greatly popular Norma Shearer in *The Latest from Paris,* a lightweight romantic comedy with Shearer and leading man Ralph Forbes as commercial travellers. Wood was then given *Telling the World,* a William Haines comedy with the young actor playing an eager fledgling newspaper reporter, cheerfully bumbling jobs in far-off places like China. Haines was a likeable, good looking player but a limited talent.

The M-G-M assignments proved to be not much better quality than those Wood had struggled with at Paramount. *So This Is College* introduced two young New York stage actors to the 1929 movie audiences, Robert Montgomery and Elliott Nugent. This was Wood's first talkie but he never allowed the dialogue to assume any importance; instead he packed the picture with dances, songs, much ribbing between the co-eds and a lot of football. *It's a Great Life* also contained plenty of songs and dances. It was an attempt to bring the Duncan Sisters from Broadway to Hollywood but the sisters soon joined the long list of stage performers who never made the celluloid grade. The film was notable for its use of colour and visual ingenuity in certain dream sequences. Wood kept the remainder of the picture moving at a fast clip, the only thing he could do with such tedious material: backstage bickerings and showbiz aspirations.

Sam Wood's efficiency may have militated against his getting worthier assignments. After ten years as a director he was well established as a man totally in command of his situations and a man who could bring in his projects on time and on budget. Perhaps his obvious enjoyment of his work led him to be considered a "workhorse." He certainly had proved time and again that he could make acceptable entertainment of the slimmest material. Wood was also called in to advise on the projects of other directors and frequently filmed sequences for which he took no credit. In the case of *They Learned about Women,* a comedy about two major league baseball stars who become vaudeville entertainers, Wood was brought in when director Jack Conway fell ill half-way through production. Hence the credit, "Directed by Jack Conway and Sam Wood," the only time Wood ever shared a credit.

The Girl Said No was another William Haines comedy; in this he was a lively, prankish young man who makes headway in the business world by trickery and charm. Wood's next film, *Sins of the Children,* was a far better property, although very heavy on sentiment. Louis Mann appeared as an old German barber living in America, a father who sacrificed everything in favour of his children, all of whom were problems to him. The youngest (Robert Montgomery) eventually made something of himself, pulled the family together and stopped the foreclosing of his father's business. The performance of German actor Mann was the film's major asset.

Sam Wood was next involved with the tragic John Gilbert. *Way for a Sailor* was Gilbert's second talkie. His first, *Redemption,* had caused considerable consternation because it revealed the actor to have a speaking voice at variance with his virile image. However, the story of John Gilbert's immediate collapse as a star has become exaggerated. He was not, as the story seems to imply, an effeminate man. His voice was light and he had a slightly mincing quality in his delivery. Unfortunately, he had enjoyed years of popularity in silent films with the dashing figure of a cavalier and the image was negated when he spoke. Had his sound films been selected more wisely Gilbert might have lasted longer, but *Way for a Sailor* was a poor choice. Here he was supposed to be a rugged seaman, matched with burly Wallace Beery as a sidekick. Wood made the film interesting with his action shots of a shipwreck and men being rescued, and glimpses of the workings of a freighter, but Gilbert was badly miscast. He made seven other pictures after this, the best being *Queen Christina* with Greta Garbo, but by 1934 he was finished. Two years later, aged forty-one, he was dead, a victim of alcohol and despair.

Wood was well represented in 1931 by four films, the best of which was *Paid*, starring the increasingly popular Joan Crawford. In this she played an innocent girl framed for a crime and jailed for three years, during which time she vows and schemes her revenge. After her release she consorts with criminals but shrewdly stays within the law, extorting money from amorous old men until she has sufficient capital to get even with the men who framed her. *Paid* was an excellent vehicle for Crawford and Wood directed it with his customary tautness; the film was made the more interesting by its insights into current prison and police methods. Wood was not so lucky with his next project, a strained comedy with William Haines, *A Tailor Made Man,* the story of a tailor's assistant who breaks into high society and reveals talent for big business. Next came a starring vehicle for young Robert Montgomery, *The Man in Possession.* It was a knockabout comedy with

Montgomery as a young man wrongly accused of a crime and jailed for a while, after which he becomes a deputy sheriff and then a butler. Montgomery could handle this kind of nonsense with ingratiating ease. The same thing could not be said of William Haines, whom Wood directed for the third, and last, time in *The New Adventures of Get-Rich-Quick Wallingford*. A very appealing player but a very limited actor Haines again played a brash young man; his Wallingford was a con-man and swindler operating in New York. It amused the audiences of the Depression, who were possibly predisposed to liking tricksters who could foil the cops and fleece the wealthy. William Haines wisely called a halt to his film career after a few more pictures like this; he went into business as an interior decorator in Beverly Hills and soon became (and still is) successful.

Ramon Novarro was the next star to be directed by Sam Wood. Like John Gilbert, Novarro had been a major box-office attraction in the Silent Era but had difficulty maintaining his popularity in talkies. He fared somewhat better than Gilbert but by the late Thirties his Hollywood career evaporated. *Huddle* presented Novarro as a fiery Italian-blooded steelworker, in love with the daughter of the boss, who goes to Yale to better himself. He there becomes a football hero, giving Wood more opportunity to indulge his flair for filming grid-iron action. The picture proved a popular feature, as did Wood's next effort, a comedy for Marie Dressler, *Prosperity*. Dressler had won an Academy Award the previous year for *Min and Bill* and M-G-M rewarded her with this starring vehicle. In this she was the president of a bank in a small town, also a mother and a widower, with the comedy arising from the complications of her job and the problems of her customers and her family. Dressler batted the material with style and Wood, now

Opposite: Madge Evans and Ramon Novarro in HUDDLE

Directing Louise Hale in THE BARBARIAN

adept at handling light comedy, kept the picture moving as quickly as possible.

Wood was again assigned a Ramon Novarro project, *The Barbarian,* an obvious attempt by M-G-M to bolster Novarro's career by returning him to the romantic-exotic image that had previously been his forte. *The Barbarian* was, in fact, a re-make of *The Arab,* a picture Novarro had made in 1924. It was also very similar to Valentino's *The Sheik.* Myrna Loy, rapidly ascending as a popular actress, played an American tourist in Egypt, travelling with her father (C. Aubrey Smith) and her *fiancé* (Reginald Denny). The *fiancé* didn't stand a chance once Loy fell prey to the charms of Novarro, a singing tourist guide but actually a prince. Glimpses of Cairo and the Egyptian desert helped to make *The Barbarian* an attractive minor package.

Wood's career advanced a step with his direction of the Clark Gable-Jean Harlow picture, *Hold Your Man,* which he also produced. The role of producer in the assembly-line days in Hollywood was largely that of supervisor rather than the supreme commander the job assumed in later years of expensive, and mostly independent, productions. Like most directors, Wood felt the irritation of supervision and he aspired to be a director-producer. A few of his best films were his own productions but in most cases the double-barrelled job was not feasible. With *Hold Your Man* Wood had a lusty property for the popular Harlow and the fast becoming popular Gable. Here they were a pair of young criminals, falling in love and trying to reform but too deep in trouble to be saved from the consequences of their misdeeds. The picture was sentimental, cheeky, wise-cracking and swiftly paced by Wood.

M-G-M gave Wood another Marie Dressler picture, co-starring her with Lionel Barrymore in *Christopher Bean,* a satire on greed. The gentleman of the title was a deceased painter whose work had no value in his lifetime but somehow assumed prestige after his

Wood watches Myrna Loy and George Brent in a scene from
STAMBOUL QUEST, with James Wong Howe at camera

death. The painter had lived in a home in which Dressler was the
maid and had painted a portrait of her, which her employers later
attempted to cajole from her. The fluff was made buoyant by the
expertise of Dressler. Wood turned from this to another exotic
vehicle featuring Myrna Loy, *Stamboul Quest*. In an absorbing little
espionage tale, Loy played an ace German spy assigned to leak
mis-information to the Allies during the Dardanelles campaign in
the First World War. Two superb villain-players helped the film:
C. Henry Gordon as the commander of Turkish forces and Lionel

Atwill as the head of the German bureau of counter-espionage. George Brent appeared as the inevitable young American falling in love and traipsing after Loy, and James Wong Howe lent the picture a certain glow with his expert photography.

Wood's only stint away from M-G-M during the Thirties was *Let 'Em Have It,* for Edward Small's Reliance company. This was a fairly conventional crime picture with Richard Arlen as a Department of Justice G-Man bearing down on the hoods of the Underworld. It was a melodrama of chase and capture, swiftly paced and highlighted by some interesting sequences showing the actual workings of detection techniques at the Department of Justice. It was characteristic of Wood to look and find ways of making a picture more interesting.

The Turning Point in the Sam Wood career now occurred. Irving Thalberg, the young and brilliant head of production at M-G-M, took it upon himself to hire the Marx Brothers. Like millions of others he had been impressed with their Paramount works but realised their progress was in doubt unless they changed the madly undisciplined structure of their films. Paramount was hesitant about renewing their contract. Thalberg asked the brothers to his office and told them he would be interested in using them provided they submitted themselves to his guidance. Since the brothers themselves were unsure of their film career and since Thalberg by 1935 had gained a reputation of near-reverence as a young "wise old man," they accepted. The first thing Thalberg did was drop young Zeppo Marx, thereby making the team a trio. The next thing was to find a director who could handle the Marx Brothers; it had to be a man who could control them without quashing them. What they needed was a paternal martinet and the man Thalberg chose was Sam Wood. Wood was not immediately interested; he considered himself a story teller and not a circus ringmaster. Thalberg won the issue when he explained to

Wood that the films he had in mind for the Marx Brothers would indeed be stories, well structured with love interest and musical numbers spacing the mad antics. *A Night at the Opera* left no doubt as to what Thalberg had in mind. In what is possibly the best of the Marx Brothers films, the audience is carried along with the comedy rather than pounded by it. One can believe in virtually all the characters in *A Night at the Opera,* which was not the case in previous Marx Brothers films. Wood was a stickler for credibility; he often said that the first thing he looked for in a script was at least one character who could be developed and brought to life before the camera.

In their book "The Marx Brothers at the Movies" (G. P. Putnam's Sons, 1968), Paul D. Zimmerman and Bert Goldblatt pointed out the strong hand of Sam Wood on *A Night at the Opera:* "Wood was a perfectionist who reshot scenes twenty or thirty times to get the one he wanted. Allan Jones believes that Wood shot so many takes because he really wasn't sure which was the best until he got the day's work into the cutting room. Unlike most directors, who supervise the cutting of the film after the entire picture has been shot, Wood edited *A Night at the Opera* day by day. This tedious retake approach, which often drove the brothers to distraction, endangered the spontaneity of the humor. But before each scene, Wood would exhort his cast to 'go in there and sell 'em a load of clams' and always managed to pull out of the clam heap a take that was funny and fresh."

The success of *A Night at the Opera* made a sequel imperative. However, Thalberg believed that the public should wait at least a year before being given another Marx Brothers epic. They were too special to overexpose. Wood was earmarked for the next picture

Wood with the Marx Brothers and Allan Jones, rehearsing the stateroom sequence in A NIGHT AT THE OPERA

Wood with Irene Franklin, Myrna Loy and Spencer Tracy
on the set of WHIPSAW

for the brothers but he needed a property in the meantime and he was assigned to direct Spencer Tracy and Myrna Loy in *Whiplash*. Again, the briskness of Wood's story-telling technique saved a conventional picture from being routine. Tracy appeared as a detective who joined a gang of jewel thieves in order to ferret them out; one of the gang was Loy, who spotted Tracy as a cop from the start but played along with him first for fun and then because of love. The by-play between Tracy and Loy was perhaps the best thing about *Whiplash*; Tracy apparently lost his temper when Wood insisted a lengthy and difficult scene for Loy be re-shot. In the opinion of the hot-tempered Tracy, Wood was too meticulous. Tracy and Wood were otherwise on friendly terms, both of them belonging to the "man's man" corner that existed at M-G-M in those days—the hunting, fishing, sports buffs like Clark Gable, Robert Taylor, Victor Fleming and Woody Van Dyke.

With the second Marx Brothers picture still not ready to go Wood directed *The Unguarded Hour,* a slick and glossy melodrama full of plot crevices, starring Loretta Young and Franchot Tone as a pair of upper crust Britons. Tone was a barrister trying a case in which his wife was a witness, but she couldn't admit being a

Wood discussing a scene for THE UNGUARDED HOUR, *with Loretta Young and Jessie Ralph*

witness because she was at the time meeting a blackmailer and paying him off in order not to reveal an old love affair that might endanger her husband's bright career. It was hokum served up with M-G-M's stylish trimmings and given added quality by such masterful character actors as Lewis Stone, Roland Young and Henry Daniell.

By the summer of 1936 *A Day at the Races* was set up and ready for production. Sam Wood moved in and took command; the Marx Brothers had tried out their material on the road, in a number of places, the film had been thoroughly mapped out by Thalberg and all signs pointed toward a splendid sequel to *Opera*. Tragedy struck M-G-M like a thunderbolt after the film had been shooting for a month: the thirty-seven-year-old Thalberg was stricken with pneumonia and died on September 14. Few film executives had ever won as much affection and respect; his loss to Hollywood was extreme. Wood had an especially warm regard for Thalberg and when he announced Thalberg's death to the cast and crew of *A Day at the Races* there were tears in his eyes. He thereupon took over the production reins of the film, in addition to direction, and completed the project as near to Thalberg's specifications as possible. As with the previous picture, the Marx antics were balanced with romance and musical numbers; Wood considered hilarity as needing occasional relief. *Races* falls a little short of *Opera* but it is still one of the better Marx Brothers pictures. Several of its scenes, notably the one in the operating room with the boys as phoney medicos examining Margaret Dumont, are considered as classic. Its most extensive musical number was particularly well staged and performed but acutely outdated: "All God's Children Got Rhythm" is tuneful and vigorously sung and danced but it has Harpo as a kind of Pied Piper leading a happy throng of Negro youngsters through a Harlemesque routine, of a kind which is now resented by black Americans.

Wood with Chico and Harpo during the shooting of
A DAY AT THE RACES

The direction of the two Marx Brothers pictures increased Wood's stock and he was thereafter handed better assignments. He also, as he wished, worked on fewer films. The next four were good pieces of entertainment but nothing memorable. *Navy Blue and Gold* was basically another college picture but this time the college was the U.S. Naval Academy at Annapolis and allowed Wood to enjoy himself staging a rousing version of the annual Army-Navy football game. The lightweight story involved James Stewart, Robert Young and Tom Brown as naval cadets of different backgrounds but similar objective—admiral's daughter Florence Rice. Such a film defies criticism, it is merely there to be enjoyed.

Wood next selected a marked change of subject, the familiar tear-jerker *Madame X.* Long a popular stage play, it had been filmed before—and it would be filmed again in 1966—this time with Gladys George as the mother who sins, suffers, grieves and sacrifices. Her performance was solid, as was the production, but it did little to advance her career other than to establish her as a character actress, at which she made a good living until her death in 1954. Gladys George was, according to Wood's two daughters, one of the few actresses to whom he took a disliking.

Wood directing his daughter, K. T. Stevens, and Tom Brown in
NAVY BLUE AND GOLD

Lynne Carver, John Beal, Gladys George, Sam Wood, and
Warren William rehearsing the concluding scene of MADAME X

Wood's two 1938 pictures had similar subject matter and both featured Mickey Rooney. *Lord Jeff* and *Stablemates* were sentimental tales about the problems of young people. The former was a story set in a Dr. Barnado's orphanage in England, this one giving lads naval training in preparation for lives at sea. Freddie Bartholemew, who had usually been cast as a nice young gentleman, here turned up as a nasty delinquent. Eventually he is brought into line and taught right from wrong as well as port from starboard. Two of his cadet chums are Rooney with an Irish

151

brogue and Peter Lawford as a cockney. Lawford, then fifteen, had just arrived in Hollywood from England, where his background was anything but cockney; he was the son of titled parents. Rooney doffed his naval uniform and turned horse lover for the next Wood project, *Stablemates*, which gave Wallace Beery top billing in his by then familiar guise as a larcenous but lovable old codger. Rooney, as a race-track waif and Beery, as an alcoholic, discredited veterinarian become pals and their friendship inspires the old man to reform. The film's best scene has Beery performing a delicate operation in a stable stall on Rooney's favourite horse while slightly drunk and worried about detection by the law. The well-staged climactic race provided Rooney with the funds for his own education as a vet. Both *Lord Jeff* and *Stablemates* might well have drowned in their own sentiment but for Wood's firm hand; he skilfully avoided bathos in all his films.

It was not until the last ten years of his life that Sam Wood really came into his own as a major film director—most of his best films appeared between 1939 and 1949. First came *Raffles*, which he directed for Samuel Goldwyn on a loanout from M-G-M. It gave David Niven one of his first starring roles, as the gentlemanly, circumspect jewel thief whose attitude toward crime in high society circles is tongue-in-cheek rather than malicious, a light-fingered Lothario who likes to foil Scotland Yard for the fun of it. The whole caper was produced with typical Goldwyn expertise although Wood is said to have considered Goldwyn more of a hindrance than a help in the actual shooting. More than one director has passed the opinion that Goldwyn performed best in his office.

Of all his films, Sam Wood's favourite was *Goodbye, Mr. Chips*, although he regarded *Kings Row* as his best work as a director. *Chips* was the only film Wood made outside the United States and it is perhaps a little ironic that a film so thoroughly English

Robert Donat—GOODBYE MR. CHIPS

in its charm and character should have been guided by a man so thoroughly American as Wood. It was, however, a film that called for a director with proven story-telling skill, a feeling for sentiment—but sentiment held in check—and an ability to deal with sensitive actors. For this Wood was the ideal choice. James Hilton's novelette, actually a 20,000 word character study of an English school master, became popular in America when it was lauded by critic Alexander Woolcott and it was Irving Thalberg

153

who astutely acquired the film rights for M-G-M. Several actors were considered for Chips, including Charles Laughton, but the choice settled on Robert Donat, who had impressed everyone with his performance as the doctor in *The Citadel*. His portrayal of Chips was flawless, as was that of Greer Garson, playing Mrs. Chips and making her screen *début*. Miss Garson had been brought to Hollywood by M-G-M a year previously, on the strength of her success on the London stage. Not being able to find any suitable roles for the ladylike Scots-Irish actress, and considering her non-commercial film material, M-G-M were about to drop their option on her. Within a few days of leaving for London, and with the role of Mrs. Chips still uncast, Wood happened to drop into a projection booth to chat with a studio executive at the moment when Greer Garson's screen test was being shown. Wood made an immediate decision to use her as the charming woman who married the shy school teacher of Brookfield and transformed him from a cold, lonely man into a warm and affable mentor to three generations of school boys.

Goodbye, Mr. Chips was one of several films M-G-M made in England in the two years prior to the Second World War. Their British operation was successful and would doubtless have continued but for the war. *Chips* called for the largest sets ever constructed for a British-made film to that time. The Brookfield exteriors were shot at Repton College, where several hundred students willingly gave up their spare time to perform as extras. The role was a *tour-de-force* for Donat, who appeared as a man in four stages of his life—at twenty-four, forty, sixty-four and eighty-three. The painstaking Wood subjected Donat to twenty-seven different moustaches before deciding on one. The time and effort produced a picture so fine it seems unreasonable to think it might have been better. It won Donat an Oscar and a nomination for Wood. He was also nominated for *Kings Row* and *Kitty Foyle* but on no occasion was Wood lucky enough to win an Academy Award.

Sam Wood returned to the M-G-M studios in Culver City in late Spring of 1939, confident of the job he had done with *Chips* and also confident that now was the time for him to strike out as an independent director. Before he left M-G-M he was called in to do a considerable amount of work on a film for which he would not receive screen credit, *Gone with the Wind*. The huge production had been in preparation and in shooting for six months and the strain had taken its toll on the leading members of the staff and the cast. It was especially hard on Victor Fleming, the vigorous and volatile director, who finally collapsed, and was confined to hospital with a nervous breakdown. Generalissimo David O. Selznick, by then greatly concerned with his costs lapping way beyond his budget, could not afford to waste a day and he called in the reliable Wood to take over from Fleming. Even when Fleming returned a month later Selznick kept Wood on hand until the end of production. Who actually was responsible for what in the vast canvas of *Gone with the Wind* is difficult to assess; Selznick and M-G-M thought it better publicity not to reveal the hodgepodge of contributions. Fleming directed the bulk of the picture but several directors were involved in many small scenes. Wood was responsible for one complete sequence—the episode involving a Yankee looter (Paul Hurst) breaking into Tara and being shot on the staircase by Scarlett—and he was partially involved in several other scenes, including the massive sequence with the hundreds of Confederate wounded in the Atlanta railroad depot.

Now free of his M-G-M contract Wood had no need to look for work. The first offer he accepted was one from Sol Lesser, who had acquired the screen rights to the Pulitzer Prize winning Thornton Wilder play, *Our Town*. It was the most distinguished property of Lesser's long career and it was to his credit that he

Guy Kibbee, Beulah Bondi, William Holden, and Thomas Mitchell in OUR TOWN

believed the unusual play should be an unusual film. The Wilder classic broke new ground in the American theatre with its simplicity, its lack of elaborate sets and scenery and the device of an on-stage narrator telling the story of two families in the New Hampshire village of Grovers Corners during the early Twentieth century, while the cast acted out the scenes. Frank Craven, the actor who had been the narrator in the Broadway presentation, was also used in the same capacity in the picture, and Thornton Wilder worked closely with Lesser and Wood to make the screen version as intelligent and touching as the stage concept. It was not the kind of vehicle that the 1940 Hollywood would have been expected to produce. In his review in the "New York Times," Bosley Crowther commented: "Sam Wood has caught in his direction all the flavor of smalltown life, with exciting visual elaborations upon the theme . . . it captures on film the simple beauties and truths of humble folks as very few pictures ever do." Aiding Wood in no small measure was the work of set designer William Cameron Menzies and a profound musical score by Aaron Copland.

The next Sam Wood picture was one that increased Ginger Rogers's esteem as an actress and brought her an Academy Award, *Kitty Foyle*. Dalton Trumbo adapted Christopher Morley's popular book, a romantic comedy about a working class Philadelphia girl who falls for a handsome socialite (Dennis Morgan) but eventually finds her happiness with a man from her own level of society (James Craig). The film has a tenderness and an intelligence rare in stories of this kind; *Kitty Foyle* was not an altogether plausible love story but it was saved from sentimentality by the playing of Rogers and the firmness of Wood's grip. Wood mapped out his films in detail and never started filming until the script was precisely what he wanted. By the end of the filming every page of his copy of the script was pencil marked with his camera angles and notes on interpretation. He was interviewed by a magazine writer during the filming of *Kitty Foyle* and he was asked to explain his technique. He had little to say about his technique other than that he considered clarity of the utmost importance and that his actors should possess at least some of the personality of the characters they portray. He also mentioned his intolerance of actors who over-act, "I find that unforgivable because it destroys realism. I don't allow scenery-chewing while emoting." Further questioned about realism in films Wood said: "You must be very careful with realism in films because it can easily be misunderstood. Every point in film story-telling must be thought of in relation to the whole. For instance, there is a scene in this picture where James Craig hires an orchestra to play until dawn so he can continue to dance with Ginger. I had to show the fatigue of the musicians, so I told them to sit back wearily and play, take their coats off, huddle in their chairs. When I began to shoot the scene I noticed one of the musicians standing while playing. I asked him why and he explained that that's what he would do if he'd been playing all night. He'd stand up from being cramped

KITTY FOYLE: Wood on the set with Ginger Rogers,
Dennis Morgan, and J. Carroll Naish

sitting down. I thought for a moment. He was right, but it seemed to me that the audience would not understand why he was standing up, so I had him sit down."

Sam Wood never allowed himself to be type-cast. He was nothing if not versatile. The three films of his which were released in 1940 substantiate this opinion: *Our Town* and *Kitty Foyle* had little in common in terms of mood and subject matter, and neither film was comparable with Wood's slam-bang western *Rangers of Fortune*. This rough-and-tumble adventure yarn had Fred Mac-Murray, Gilbert Roland and Albert Dekker as good-bad roustabouts who escape a Mexican firing squad in the wake of a gun running escapade and then become Robin Hood-like bandits in Texas. The trio adopt an orphaned moppet and then proceed spectacularly to erase the villains responsible for making her an orphan. Wood's wild western was almost a parody on the *genre* but he never allowed it to lapse into complete buffoonery. Wood was blessed with one of the most valuable assets of film story-telling—a sense of balance.

With the exception of the two Marx Brothers pictures, the best comedy directed by Sam Wood was *The Devil and Miss Jones*. The original screenplay by Norman Krasna had a strong flavour of social satire in its bones, and the film was lifted by the performances of Jean Arthur as a department store sales-girl who leads a strike against her employer, and Charles Coburn as the employer, a tight, irascible old tycoon who learns humility when he takes a job as a clerk in his own store in order to find out what is going on. The script, the direction and the performances blended into a delightful product. Especially effective were the scenes in which the crusty tycoon became familiar with the character of his employees, some of them kindly, some petty but all of them leading lives greatly different from his own. He joins them on a picnic jaunt to packed Coney Island and he finally takes part in

Edmund Gwenn, Jean Arthur, and Charles Coburn in
THE DEVIL AND MISS JONES

a parade to picket himself. Coburn was superb, and Jean Arthur, possibly the deftest and most appealing of Hollywood's comediennes, made the film one of her best. Perhaps the fact that *The Devil and Miss Jones* was produced by her husband, Frank Ross, might have had some bearing on the matter. Again Wood kept the farce in balance, pacing it and controlling it to give it a consistent buoyancy.

Charles Coburn was well in evidence in Wood's next film, the prestigious *Kings Row,* but in a greatly different guise. His sadistic small-town surgeon in this impressive filming of the Henry Bellamann novel was among the blackest characters in screen literature. It was this evil character who unnecessarily amputated the legs of a handsome young man (Ronald Reagan) as punishment for what he considered wickedness, thereby causing his smitten young daughter (Nancy Coleman) to become neurotic and unbalanced. This was one of several dark episodes in a peculiarly sombre but highly artistic piece of film-making.

Ronald Reagan and Robert Cummings in KINGS ROW

Kings Row was completed by Warner Brothers by the end of 1941 but they delayed its release for some months, being doubtful about its prospects with wartime audiences. The film was certainly not everyone's cup of tea; it did moderately well but it took time for *Kings Row* to build up the appreciation that eventually registered it as a major achievement in cinematic art. It was a lengthy, convoluted film that called for the talent of an imaginative but level-headed director, one with as much sense of discipline as story-telling technique. That Wood performed the job admirably there is no question but it must be conceded that in giving *Kings Row* its classical proportions he was helped by three superb artists: William Cameron Menzies, James Wong Howe, and Erich Wolfgang Korngold. Wood had first worked with Menzies on *Gone with the Wind;* the two became friends, and Menzies was the production designer on most of Wood's subsequent pictures. *Kings Row* was filmed almost entirely on sound stages at the Warner Brothers studios in Burbank and it was Menzies's rich and melodramatic settings that gave the film its feel. In James Wong Howe Wood had a cinematographer of genius; with his lighting and his movements Howe literally created drama. And in his musical scoring Korngold deepened the film's moods and swayed its emotions. The Austrian composer had excelled in the field of opera and his music for *Kings Row* is virtually opera minus singing. However, it was Sam Wood who guided all these elements and moulded them into a fascinating portrait of love, hate, madness, tragedy and happiness in the life of an American town around the turn-of-the-century. *Kings Row* will doubtless continue to be one of the prime choices among students and lovers of film.

Wood began his work on *For Whom the Bell Tolls* while still involved in making *Kings Row*. At the end of a day at Warners he would proceed in the evening to Paramount to discuss production plans for filming the Hemingway book. However, it became

Gary Cooper with Babe Ruth in THE PRIDE OF THE YANKEES

necessary for him to drop the project and proceed with *The Pride of the Yankees*, the story of baseball star Lou Gehrig. It was an ideal vehicle for Gary Cooper, who was himself a kind of idealisation of the American male. The modest and likeable Gehrig had an amazing career with the New York Yankees; between 1923 and 1939 he played more than two thousand consecutive games and was idolised by the fans. He retired when stricken with amytropic lateral sclerosis and he died in 1941, aged thirty-seven. *The Pride of the Yankees* was an excellent film and in Cooper and Wood it

Wood briefs Ingrid Bergman and Gary Cooper before the sleeping bag scene in FOR WHOM THE BELL TOLLS

found the perfect actor and the perfect director.

For Whom the Bell Tolls was the major project of Sam Wood's career, the one on which he spent the most time and the greatest effort. He produced as well as directed this epic story of the Spanish Civil War and it was a project in which he thoroughly believed. The Loyalist hero of Ernest Hemingway's book—Robert Jordan— was a political idealisation of direct appeal to Wood. Hemingway felt, and everyone agreed, that the actor to play Jordan was Gary Cooper. Cooper, however, was contracted to Samuel Goldwyn and in order to get the actor Wood had to agree to direct him in *The Pride of the Yankees* before he appeared in *Bell*. Wood had actually done several months work on *Bell* in late 1941, filming non-Jordan sequences in winter locations in the High Sierra Nevada Mountains of northern California. Wood halted production on *Bell*, filmed the Goldwyn picture and resumed production the following June. Due to wartime restrictions placing a limit on the amount of money that could be used on new construction material—five thousand dollars per film—the decision was made to film most of the picture on location in the Sonora Pass district of the Sierras. Wood later wrote: "I have never experienced anything as difficult as filming under the conditions we had, at an elevation of ten thousand feet, scrambling over rocks. We even uprooted wildflowers and greenery to prevent the harsh landscape from becoming 'pretty' for the Technicolor camera and we substituted ancient, gnarled tree trunks instead. Due to the quartz and metallic content of the rocks, painters had to spray down the backgrounds of almost all the exteriors. Not only did we go to the mountain but we painted it too." The company were on the location until the first week of September, then returned to the studios at Paramount in Hollywood and the shooting was completed by the end of October.

Wood's sense of casting was invariably good but he made an error in picking Vera Zorina to play the role of Maria. The popular choice, even in Wood's own family, was Ingrid Bergman but Wood himself was adamant in thinking Zorina was the better choice. He took the German-born ballet dancer-actress with him to the location but after a week of shooting he conceded that she was not right for the part and sent for Bergman. Critical reaction to *For Whom the Bell Tolls* was mixed; it was admired by all for its spectacular settings and photography but many felt that the love interest was overplayed, making the issue of the war almost secondary, and that it dragged in places. Three hours in its first issue, Wood later cut the picture by half an hour and when reissued a few years after his death it was considerably truncated. To what must have been his bitter disappointment, Wood was not nominated for an Academy Award although his photographer (Ray Rennahan), his art director (William Cameron Menzies), his editors (Sherman Todd and John Link), his composer (Victor Young) and his four leading players (Cooper, Bergman, Akim Tamiroff and Katina Paxinou) did receive nominations. But only Paxinou actually won an Oscar.

The teaming of Gary Cooper and Ingrid Bergman was assumed by Hollywood to be an exciting potential. Immediately the two stars and Sam Wood finished *For Whom the Bell Tolls* they moved to the Warner Brothers studios in Burbank to negotiate the filming of Edna Ferber's *Saratoga Trunk*. The business details were quickly attended to and Wood started filming the expensive and lavish property in late February, 1943. The end result was a considerable disappointment: the love story of a tempestuous New Orleans courtesan and a Texas cowboy failed to generate sparks, despite the film's rich production values. Admirable but dull was the critical consensus, and in its languid pacing the long story seemed even longer. It showed none of the briskness that usually characterised Wood's directing, except in a late scene involving a train wreck and a brawl between rival railroad gangs. The Cooper-Bergman pairing soon dissolved and Warners, possibly wisely, delayed the release of *Saratoga Trunk* for two full years, except for showings to servicemen on overseas locations. The Warner decision was also probably influenced by *For Whom the Bell Tolls* being not quite the box-office blockbuster everyone thought it would be. In spite of all this, the mutual regard between Cooper and Wood remained high and firm, and the two men immediately launched into another project, *Casanova Brown*. Both realised that a change of material was needed, something light in contrast to

Ingrid Bergman and Gary Cooper in SARATOGA TRUNK

the epic and heroic dimensions of their three previous pictures. *Casanova Brown* was an amusing fable of a young man who kidnaps his newborn daughter by a former marriage on the eve of his nuptials with another spouse, in order to save the child from being put up for adoption. The film was clearly aimed at the female movie market and permitted Cooper to display his talent for restrained comedy; he was seen as a serious-minded fellow feeding the baby her formula as if he were conducting a major medical operation. Wood played all the situations and characters to the hilt but *Casanova Brown* was only a middling success.

The next two Sam Wood pictures were also comedies, *Guest Wife* and *Heartbeat,* but they are no mightier as audience pleasers than *Casanova Brown.* Claudette Colbert was the major asset of *Guest Wife,* a trifle about a wife who agrees to pose as the wife of her husband's best friend, in order that he might keep his job with an employer who prefers his employees to be married. The same script today might pass as a ninety-minute TV film, provided it was graced with the charm and expertise of a Colbert. As a director Wood was especially good with actors, he knew how to handle them and how to get the best from them and that in itself is a talent. He never agreed with the many directors who considered actors as puppets; each Wood filming began with a casual discussion with his players as to how they saw their parts. Frequently, with actors who differed with his own concept, he would shoot a scene both ways and later in the projection room explain why his own handling was necessary to the construction of the film. Wood was the most diplomatic of dictators.

Ginger Rogers, who had performed well by Wood with his *Kitty Foyle,* accepted his invitation to star in *Heartbeat,* a whimsical treatment of larceny and a re-make of a French picture of prewar years. The Hollywood version lacked Gallic charm but it had a few points in its favour, among them Basil Rathbone as a magisterial modern day Fagin running a school for pickpockets in Paris. Rogers became a pupil after escaping from a reformatory, and later a pawn of shifty diplomat Adolphe Menjou but she was too good-hearted to be a real criminal. As more than one critic pointed out, *Heartbeat* needed the sly touch of a Guitry or a Lubitsch, not the open-handed humour of Wood.

Wood turned his back on comedy, as well he might, and decided on a stylish melodrama for his next project. *Ivy,* made in 1947, still has its supporters, people who consider it a minor cinematic masterpiece, thereby differing from others who find it somewhat dull. Wood produced the picture in association with the veteran William Cameron Menzies, who clearly gave the film its handsome turn-of-the-century English mountings. Joan Fontaine ably performed the title role, that of a beauteous murderess, gorgeously gowned and elegant of manner, who kills to advance her wealth and place in society. She meets her justified end plunging down a lift shaft. The film was strong on moods and mystery and movement but there were those who felt Wood was too obvious in his story telling, that more subtlety on his part would have produced an even better film.

Command Decision was a perfect vehicle for Sam Wood's thoroughly masculine, no-nonsense style of film-making. The stage play of the same name by William Wister Haines about the anguish of command in wartime aviation was transferred to the screen with little change and an admirable restraint on the part of M-G-M not to embellish it with combat footage. The story limits itself in the main to the offices of the officers who mapped out and desk-commanded the bombing raids over Germany by the U.S. Eighth Army Air Corps. *Command Decision* needed the firm hand of a man like Wood to command the large all-male cast headed by Clark Gable, Van Johnson, Walter Pidgeon, Brian Donlevy and Charles Bickford. Wood's film was a kind of updated aerial version of *Journey's End,* grimly humorous and fairly honest in revealing the almost dehumanising function of operating a modern war machine. Wood gave the story the proper blend of tough-mindedness and sentiment, pulling no punches in showing the devious expediences and opportunism as well as heroism and heartfelt concern among the various militarists and politicians. Clark Gable was at ease in the uniform of a Brigadier-General,

COMMAND DECISION: *Clark Gable, Walter Pidgeon,*
Charles Bickford

having himself served as a combat officer with the American air force. He held his own as the lead player but it must have been difficult for him to handle the lengthy dialogue in what was largely a filmed play. Gable, never a devotee of the art of acting and many years removed from his early days on the stage, excelled in the one sequence of *Command Decision* written especially for the film version, where he stands on the balcony of a control tower and "talks down" a crippled Flying Fortress.

The Stratton Story was another perfect vehicle for Wood; by this time in his career there was no doubt about his ability to direct a film about sport, especially baseball. His own interest in sport carried over into such pictures yet he was always able to cut off sentiment before it became maudlin. In other hands *The Stratton Story* might have been very maudlin; it told the true story—and kept to the facts—about Monty Stratton, an American farmer with a passion for baseball, who became a major league player and lost a leg in a hunting accident. Rather than quit the game Stratton surmounted the obstacle of an artificial leg and continued his career

Wood with June Allyson and Agnes Moorehead while shooting
THE STRATTON STORY

as an ace pitcher. With James Stewart giving a knowing performance as the homespun and gutsy Stratton, and June Allyson as Mrs. Stratton, the film could hardly fail to be a winner, at least in the United States.

Sam Wood's final film was a western, made largely on location in New Mexico, *Ambush* starring Robert Taylor as an army scout on duty with a cavalry command during a campaign against the Apaches. It was mostly a routine Grade A western, made with Wood's well-tried theory, "If it isn't too good, keep it moving." *Ambush* certainly moved; horses leapt and galloped, cavalrymen and Indians bit the dust in rapid order, and dozens of characters were shot, scalped or chased. Soldiers wiped out Indians and vice versa, and the customers were well satisfied. Wood considered it as just one more assignment. Unfortunately, it was his last.

Wood completed *Ambush* at the M-G-M studios in the middle of September 1949, and then began setting up his next film, *No Sad Songs for Me,* to be filmed at Columbia and to star Margaret Sullavan. On the evening of September 22, at the offices of the Motion Picture Alliance, he was stricken with a heart attack and died a few hours later in hospital. Wood founded the Motion Picture Alliance in 1944 and was its first president; it was an anti-Communist organisation formed of members from management and labour in the film industry and it was dedicated to seeking out and expelling those people whom it considered traitorous to American interests. While Sam Wood had been noted for most of his years in Hollywood as an even tempered man with an absolute catholicity of taste in his life style and his work, the political sentiments revealed in his last few years brought forth a well voiced anger that disappointed some of his friends and greatly concerned his family.

In the opinion of his daughter, actress K. T. Stevens: "I think two things contributed to my father's death at sixty-five. One was the energy he burned up while making *Ambush* on location; they were at an elevation of nine thousand feet for several weeks and Dad never stopped. He was always very active. On location he was the first up in the morning and the younger actors were amazed at the way he ran around all day. The second thing was politics. His anger was so deep he seethed with it and I believe it affected his health."

Hollywood turned out to honour Sam Wood at his funeral. Among his pallbearers were Clark Gable, Dore Schary, William Cameron Menzies and Louis B. Mayer. Wood's death meant little to the public but it marked the end of a long and respectable film career. Wood had been in the business for forty years and he had seen it grow from infancy to a major industry. Rarely did he show signs of brilliance yet he was never at any time less than thoroughly professional. The work is the man: Sam Wood was uncomplicated, self-assured, clear minded and he enjoyed working. In so far as he understood it, he was a master of his craft.

SAM WOOD Filmography

DOUBLE SPEED (1920). Sc: Byron Morgan. With Wallace Reid ("Speed" Carr), Wanda Hawley (Sallie McPherson), Tully Marshall (Donald McPherson), Theodore Roberts (John Ogden), Lucien Littlefield, Guy Oliver. Prod: Paramount-Artcraft.

EXCUSE MY DUST (1920). Sc: Byron Morgan (from his story "The Bear Trap"). With Wallace Reid ("Toodles" Walton), Tully Marshall (President Muchler), Ann Little (Dorothy Walden), Guy Oliver (Darley), Otto Brower (Henderson), Theodore Roberts, Walter Long, Byron Morgan, Will M. Ritchey, William Wallace Reid Jr., James Gordon, Fred Huntley, Jack Herbert. Prod: Paramount-Artcraft.

THE DANCIN' FOOL (1920). Sc: Clara G. Kennedy (story by Henry Payson Dowst). With Wallace Reid (Sylvester Tibble), Bebe Daniels (Junie Budd), Raymond Hatton (Enoch Jones), Willis Marks (Meeks), George B. Williams (McGammon), Lillian Leighton, Tully Marshall, Ernest Joy, Carlos San Martin, W. H. Brown, Ruth Ashby. Presented by Jesse L. Lasky for Paramount-Artcraft.

SICK ABED (1920). Sc: Clara G. Kennedy (play by Ethel Watts Mumford). With Wallace Reid (Reginald Jay), Bebe Daniels (Nurse Durant), Tully Marshall (Chalmers), John Steppling (John Weems), Winifred Greenwood (Constance Weems), Clarence Geldart, Lucien Littlefield, Robert Bolder, Lorenza Lazzarini, George Kuwa.

Presented by Jesse L. Lasky for Paramount-Artcraft.

WHAT'S YOUR HURRY? (1920). Sc: Byron Morgan (from his story, "The Hippopotamus Parade"). With Wallace Reid (Dusty Rhoades), Lois Wilson (Virginia MacMurran), Charles Ogle (Patrick MacMurran), Clarence Burton (Brenton Harding), Ernest Butterworth (Office Boy), Jack Young. Presented by Jesse L. Lasky for Paramount-Artcraft.

A CITY SPARROW (1920). Sc: Clara G. Kennedy (story by Kate Jordan). With Ethel Clayton (Milly West), Walter Hiers (Tim Ennis), Clyde Fillmore (David Muir), Lillian Leighton (Ma Ennis), William Boyd (Hughie Ray), Rose Cade, Robert Brower, Helen Jerome Eddy, Sylvia Ashton. Presented by Jesse L. Lasky for Paramount-Artcraft.

HER BELOVED VILLAIN (1920). Sc: Alice Eyton (play "La veglione" by Bisson and Carré). With Wanda Hawley (Suzanne Bergamot), Ramsay Wallace (Paul Blythe), Templer Powell (Louis Martinot), Tully Marshall (Dr. Joseph Poulard), Lillian Leighton (Madame Poulard), Gertrude Claire, Robert Bolder, Margaret McWade, Irma Coonly, Jay Peters. Prod: Realart.

HER FIRST ELOPEMENT (1920). Sc: Edith Kennedy (story by Alice Duer Miller). With Wanda Hawley (Christina Elliott), Jerome Patrick (Adrian Maitland), Nell Craig (Lotta St. Regis), Lucien Littlefield (Ted Maitland), Jay Eaton (Gerald Elliott), Helen Dunbar,

Herbert Standing, Edwin Stevens, Margaret Morris, Ann Hastings, John MacKinnon. *Prod:* Realart.

THE SNOB (1921). *Sc:* Alice Eyton (story by William J. Neidig). *Ph:* Albert Gilks. *With* Wanda Hawley (*Kathryn Haynes*), Edwin Stevens (*Jim Haynes*), Walter Hiers (*Pud Welland*), Sylvia Ashton (*Mrs. Haynes*), William E. Lawrence (*Capt. William Putnam*), Julia Faye (*Betty Welland*), Richard Wayne, Josephine Cromwell, Althea Worthley. *Prod:* Realart Pictures. 5r.

PECK'S BAD BOY (1921). *Sc:* Sam Wood (adapted from stories by George Wilbur Peck). *Titles:* Irvin S. Cobb. *Ph:* Albert Gilks, Harry Hallenberger. *With* Jackie Coogan (*Peck's Bad Boy*), Wheeler Oakman (*The Man in the Case*), Doris May (*The Girl in the Case*), Raymond Hatton (*The Village Grocer*), Lillian Leighton (*Ma Peck*), James Corrigan (*Pa Peck*), Charles Hatton, Gloria Wood, Queenie. *Prod:* Irving M. Lesser. *Dist:* Associated First National Pictures. 5r.

THE GREAT MOMENT (1921). *Sc:* Monte M. Katterjohn (story by Elinor Glyn). *Ph:* Albert Gilks. *With* Gloria Swanson (*Nada Pelham/Nadine Pelham*), Alec B. Francis (*Sir Edward Pelham*), Milton Sills (*Bayard Delavel*), F. R. Butler (*Eustace*), Arthur Hull (*Hopper*), Raymond Brathwayt, Helen Dunbar, Clarence Geldart, Julia Faye, Ann Grigg. Presented by Jesse L. Lasky for Famous Players-Lasky. *Dist:* Paramount. 7r.

UNDER THE LASH [GB: THE SHULAMITE] (1921). *Sc:* J. E. Nash (story by Claude and Alice Askew, and play by Claude Askew and Edward Knob-

lock). *Ph:* Albert Gilks. *Asst. dir:* A. R. Hamm. *With* Gloria Swanson (*Deborah Krillet*), Mahlon Hamilton (*Robert Waring*), Russell Simpson (*Simeon Krillet*), Lillian Leighton (*Tant Anna Vanderberg*), Lincoln Stedman (*Jan Vanderberg*), Thena Jasper, Clarence Ford. Presented by Jesse L. Lasky for Famous Players-Lasky. *Dist:* Paramount. 6r.

DON'T TELL EVERYTHING (1921). *Sc:* Albert Shelley Le Vino (story by Lorna Moon). *Ph:* Albert Gilks. *Asst. dir:* A. R. Hamm. *With* Wallace Reid (*Cullen Dale*), Gloria Swanson (*Marian Westover*), Elliott Dexter (*Harvey Gilroy*), Dorothy Cumming (*Jessica Ramsey*), Genevieve Blinn (*Mrs. Morgan*), Gloria Wood, De Briac Twins. Presented by Jesse L. Lasky for Famous Players-Lasky. *Dist:* Paramount. 5r.

BEYOND THE ROCKS (1922). *Sc:* Jack Cunningham (story by Elinor Glyn). *Ph:* Albert Gilks. *With* Gloria Swanson (*Theodora Fitzgerald*), Rudolph Valentino (*Lord Bracondale*), Edythe Chapman (*Lady Bracondale*), Alec B. Francis (*Captain Fitzgerald*), Robert Bolder (*Josiah Brown*), Gertrude Astor, Mabel Van Buren, Helen Dunbar, F. R. Butler, Raymond Brathwayt, June Elvidge. Presented by Jesse L. Lasky for Famous Players-Lasky. *Dist:* Paramount. 7r.

HER GILDED CAGE (1922). *Sc:* Elmer Harris, Percy Heath (play "The Gilded Cage" by Anne Nichols). *Ph:* Albert Gilks. *With* Gloria Swanson (*Suzanne Ornoff*), David Powell (*Arnold Pell*), Harrison Ford (*Lawrence Pell*), Anne Cornwall (*Jacqueline Ornoff*), Walter Hiers (*Bud Walton*), Charles Stevenson. Presented by Jesse

L. Lasky for Famous Players-Lasky. *Dist:* Paramount. 6r.

THE IMPOSSIBLE MRS. BELLEW (1922). *Sc:* Percy Heath, Monte M. Katterjohn (play by David Lisle). *Ph:* Albert Gilks. *With* Gloria Swanson (*Betty Bellew*), Robert Cain (*Lance Bellew*), Conrad Nagel (*John Helston*)°, Richard Wayne (*Jerry Woodruff*), Frank Elliott (*Count Radisloff*)°, Gertrude Astor, June Elvidge, Herbert Standing, Mickey Moore, Helen Dunbar, Arthur Hull, Clarence Burton, Pat Moore. Presented by Jesse L. Lasky for Famous Players-Lasky. *Dist:* Paramount. 8r.

MY AMERICAN WIFE (1923). *Sc:* Monte M. Katterjohn (story by Hector Turnbull). *Ph:* Albert Gilks. *With* Gloria Swanson (*Natalie Chester*), Antonio Moreno (*Manuel La Tassa*)°, Josef Swickard (*Don Fernando De Contas*), Eric Mayne (*Carlos De Grossa*), Gino Corrado (*Pedro De Grossa*), Edythe Chapman, Aileen Pringle, Walter Long, F. R. Butler, Jacques D'Auray, Loyal Underwood, Mary Land. Presented by Jesse L. Lasky for Famous Players-Lasky. *Dist:* Paramount.

PRODIGAL DAUGHTERS (1923). *Sc:* Monte M. Katterjohn (novel by Joseph Hocking). *Ph:* Albert Gilks. *With* Gloria Swanson (*Elinor "Swiftie" Forbes*), Ralph Graves (*Roger Corbin*), Vera Reynolds (*Marjory Forbes*), Theodore Roberts (*J. D. Forbes*), Louise Dresser (*Mrs. Forbes*), Charles Clary, Robert Agnew, Maude Wayne, Jiquel Lenoe, Eric Mayne, Antonio Corsi. Presented by Jesse L. Lasky for Famous Players-Lasky. *Dist:* Paramount. 6r.

BLUEBEARD'S EIGHTH WIFE (1923). *Sc:* Sada Cowan (play "La huitième femme de Barbe Bleue" by Alfred Savoire, translated by Charlton Andrews). *Ph:* Albert Gilks. *With* Gloria Swanson (*Mona De Briac*), Huntley Gordon (*John Brandon*), Charles Green (*Robert*), Lianne Salvor (*Lucienne*), Paul Weigel (*Marquis De Briac*), F. R. Butler (*Lord Henry Seville*), Robert Agnew, Irene Dalton, Majel Coleman, Thais Valdemar. Presented by Jesse L. Lasky for Famous Players-Lasky. *Dist:* Paramount. 6r. Re-made in 1938 by Ernst Lubitsch.

HIS CHILDREN'S CHILDREN (1923). *Sc:* Monte M. Katterjohn (novel by Arthur Chesney Train). *Ph:* Albert Gilks. *With* Bebe Daniels (*Diana*), Dorothy Mackaill (*Sheila*), James Rennie (*Lloyd Maitland*), George Fawcett (*Peter B. Kayne*), Hale Hamilton (*Rufus Kayne*), Katheryn Lean, Mahlon Hamilton, Mary Eaton, Warner Oland, John Davidson, Sally Crute, Joseph Burke, Templer Powell, Lawrence D'Orsay, Dora Mills Adams, H. Cooper Cliffe. Presented by Adolph Zukor for Famous Players-Lasky. *Dist:* Paramount. 8r.

THE NEXT CORNER (1924). *Sc:* Monte M. Katterjohn (play and novel by Kate Jordan). *Ph:* Albert Gilks. *With* Conway Tearle (*Robert Maury*), Dorothy Mackaill (*Elsie Maury*), Lon Chaney (*Juan Serafin*), Ricardo Cortez (*Don Arturo*), Louise Dresser (*Nina Race*), Remea Radzina, Dorothy Cumming, Mrs. Bertha Felucha, Bernard Seigel. Presented by Jesse L. Lasky, Adolph Zukor for Famous Players-Lasky. *Dist:* Paramount. 7r.

BLUFF (1924). *Sc:* Willis Goldbeck (story by Rita Weisman, Josephine L. Quirk). *Ph:* Albert Gilks. *With* Agnes

Ayres (*Betty Hallowell*), Antonio Moreno (*Robert Fitzmaurice*), Fred Butler (*"Boss" Mitchell*), Clarence Burton (*Jack Hallowell*), Pauline Paquette (*Fifine*), Jack Gardner, Arthur Hoyt, E. H. Calvert, Roscoe Karns. Presented by Jesse L. Lasky, Adolph Zukor for Famous Players-Lasky. *Dist:* Paramount. 6r.

THE FEMALE (1924). *Sc:* Agnes Christine Johnson (story "Dalla, the Lion Cub" by Cynthia Stockley). *Ph:* Albert Gilks. *With* Betty Compson (*Dalla*), Warner Baxter (*Col. Valentine*), Noah Beery (*Barend de Beer*), Dorothy Cumming (*Clodah Harrison*), Freeman Wood (*Clon Biron*), Helen Butler, Pauline French, Edgar Norton, Florence Wix. Presented by Jesse L. Lasky for Famous Players-Lasky. *Dist·* Paramount. 7r.

THE MINE WITH THE IRON DOOR (1924). *Sc:* Arthur Statter, Mary Alice Scully (novel by Harold Bell Wright, adapted by Hope Loring, Louis D. Lighton). *Ph:* Glen MacWilliams. *With* Pat O'Malley (*Hugh Edwards*), Dorothy Mackaill (*Marta*), Raymond Hatton (*Bill Jansen*), Charlie Murray (*Thad Grove*)°, Bert Woodruff (*Bob Hill*)°, Mitchell Lewis, Mary Carr, William Collier Jr., Creighton Hale, Robert Frazer, Clarence Burton, Lillian Leighton, Marie Eagle Eye, Laura Winston, Fred Huntley. *Prod:* Irving [Sol] M. Lesser for Sol Lesser Productions. *Dist:* Principal Pictures. 8r.

THE RE-CREATION OF BRIAN KENT (1925). *Sc:* Arthur Statter, Mary Alice Scully (novel by Harold Bell Wright). *Ph:* Glen MacWilliams. *With* Kenneth Harlan (*Brian Kent*), Helene

Chadwick (*Betty Joe*), Mary Carr (*Auntie Sue*), Zasu Pitts (*Judy*), Rosemary Theby (*Mrs. Kent*), T. Roy Barnes (*Harry Green*), Ralph Lewis, Russell Simpson, De Witt Jennings, Russell Powell. *Prod:* Irving M. Lesser for Sol Lesser Productions. *Dist:* Principal Pictures. 7r.

FASCINATING YOUTH (1926). *Sc:* Paul Schofield (story by Byron Morgan). *Ph:* Leo Tover. *With* Charles Rogers (*Teddy Ward*), Ivy Harris (*Jeanne King*), Jack Luden (*Ross Page*), Walter Goss (*Randy Furness*), Claud Buchanan (*Bobby Stearns*), Mona Palma, Thelma Todd, Josephine Dana, Thelda Kenvin, Jeanne Morgan, Dorothy Nourse, Irving Hartley, Gregory Blackton, Robert Andrews, Charles Brokaw, Iris Gray, Ralph Lewis, Joseph Burke, James Bradbury Snr., Harry Sweet, William Black, Richard Dix, Adolphe Menjou, Clara Bow, Lois Wilson, Percy Marmont, Chester Conklin, Thomas Meighan, Lila Lee, Lewis Milestone, Mal St. Clair. Presented by Adolph Zukor, Jesse L. Lasky for Famous Players-Lasky. *Dist:* Paramount. 7r.

ONE MINUTE TO PLAY (1926). *Sc:* Byron Morgan. *Ph:* Charles G. Clarke. *Asst. dir:* Jack McKeown. *With* Harold "Red" Grange (*Red Wade*), Mary McAllister (*Sally Rogers*), Charles Ogle (*John Wade*), George Wilson (*Player 33*), Ben Hendricks Jr. (*Biff Wheeler*), Lee Shumway, Al Cooke, Kit Guard, King Tut, Lincoln Stedman, Jay Hunt, Edythe Chapman. Presented by Joseph P. Kennedy for R-C Pictures. *Dist:* Film Booking Offices of America. 8r.

ROOKIES (1927). *Sc:* Byron Morgan.

177

Ph: Ira Morgan. *Titles:* Joe Farnham. *Sets:* Cedric Gibbons, David Townsend. *Ed:* Conrad Nervig. *With* Karl Dane (*Sgt. Diggs*), George K. Arthur (*Greg Lee*), Marceline Day (*Betty Wayne*), Louise Lorraine (*Zella Fay*), Frank Currier (*The Judge*), E. H. Calvert, Tom O'Brien, Charles Sullivan, Lincoln Stedman, Gene Stone. *Prod:* M-G-M. 7r.

A RACING ROMEO (1927). *Sc:* Byron Morgan. *Ph:* Charles G. Clarke. *Asst. dir:* Jack McKeown. *With* Harold "Red" Grange (*Red Walden*), Jobyna Ralston (*Sally*), Trixie Friganza (*Aunt Hattie*), Walter Hiers (*Sparks*), Ben Hendricks Jr. (*Rube Oldham*), Warren Rogers, Ashton Dearholt, Marjorie Zier. Presented by Joseph P. Kennedy for R-C Pictures. *Dist:* Film Booking Offices of America. 7r.

THE FAIR CO-ED (1927). *Sc:* Byron Morgan (play by George Ade). *Ph:* John Seitz. *Art dir:* Cedric Gibbons, Arnold Gillespie. *Ed:* Conrad A. Nervig. *With* Marion Davies (*Marion*), Johnny Mack Brown (*Bob Dixon*), Jane Winton (*Betty*), Thelma Hill (*Rose*), Lillian Leighton (*Housekeeper*), Gene Stone, Joel McCrea [extra]. *Prod:* M-G-M. 7r.

THE LATEST FROM PARIS (1928). *Sc:* A. P. Younger (from his own story). *Ph:* William Daniels. *Titles:* Joe Farnham. *Sets:* Cedric Gibbons, Arnold Gillespie. *Ed:* Basil Wrangell. *With* Norma Shearer (*Ann Dolan*), George Sidney (*Sol Blogg*), Ralph Forbes (*Joe Adams*), Tenen Holtz (*Abe Littauer*), William Bakewell (*Bud Dolan*), Margaret Landis, Bert Roach. *Prod:* M-G-M. 8r.

TELLING THE WORLD (1928). *Sc:* Raymond L. Schrock (story by Dale

Van Every). *Ph:* William Daniels. *Titles:* Joe Farnham. *Art dir:* Cedric Gibbons. *Ed:* Margaret Booth, John Colton. *With* William Haines (*Don Davis*), Anita Page (*Chrystal Malone*), Eileen Percy (*Maizie*), Frank Currier (*Mr. Davis*), Polly Moran (*Landlady*), Bert Roach (*Lane*), William V. Mong, Mathew Betz. *Prod:* M-G-M. 8r.

SO THIS IS COLLEGE (1929). *Sc:* Al Boasberg, Delmer Daves. *Ph:* Leonard Smith. *Art dir:* Cedric Gibbons. *Ed:* Frank Sullivan, Leslie F. Wilder. *Music:* Martin Broones. *With* Elliott Nugent (*Eddie*), Robert Montgomery (*Biff*), Cliff Edwards (*Windy*), Sally Starr (*Babs*), Phyllis Crane (*Betty*), Dorothy Dehn (*Jane*), Max Davidson, Ann Brody, Oscar Rudolph, Gene Stone, Polly Moran, Lee Shumway, Delmer Daves. *Prod:* M-G-M. 11r.

IT'S A GREAT LIFE (1929). *Sc. and comedy dial:* Al Boasberg. *Dial:* Willard Mack. (story by Byron Morgan, Alfred Block). *Ph:* J. Peverell Marley. *Art dir:* Cedric Gibbons. *Ed:* Frank Sullivan. *With* Rosetta Duncan (*Casey Hogan*), Vivian Duncan (*Babe Hogan*), Lawrence Gray (*Jimmy Dean*), Jed Prouty (*Mr. Parker*), Benny Rubin (*Benny Friedman*). *Prod:* M-G-M. Part Technicolor. 11r.

THEY LEARNED ABOUT WOMEN (1930). *Co-dir:* Jack Conway. *Sc:* Sarah Y. Mason. *Dial:* Arthur "Bugs" Baer (story by A. P. Younger). *Ph:* Leonard Smith. *Art dir:* Cedric Gibbons. *Ed:* James McKay, Thomas Held. *With* Joseph T. Schenck (*Jack*), Gus Van (*Jerry*), Bessie Love (*Mary*), Mary Doran (*Daisy*), J. C. Nugent (*Stafford*), Tom Dugan (*Tim*), Eddie Gribbon,

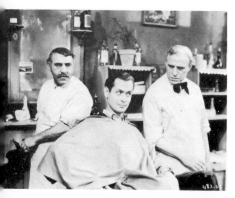

Henry Armetta, Robert Montgomery, and Louis Mann in SINS OF THE CHILDREN

Benny Rubin, Francis X. Bushman Jr. *Prod:* M-G-M. 11r.

THE GIRL SAID NO (1930). *Sc:* Sarah Y. Mason. *Dial:* Charles MacArthur (story by A. P. Younger). *Ph:* Ira Morgan. *Art dir:* Cedric Gibbons. *Ed:* Frank Sullivan, Truman E. Wood, George Boemler. *Songs:* Martin Broones, Fred Fisher. *With* William Haines (*Tom Ward*), Leila Hyams (*Mary Howe*), Polly Moran (*Hildegarde*), Marie Dressler (*Hettie Brown*), Francis X. Bushman Jr. (*McAndrews*), Clara Blandick, William Janney, William V. Mong, Junior Coghlan, Phyllis Crane. *Prod:* M-G-M. 10r.

SINS OF THE CHILDREN [GB: THE RICHEST MAN IN THE WORLD] (1930). *Sc:* Samuel Ornitz. *Dial:* Elliott Nugent, Clara Lipman (story "Fa-

ther's Day" by Elliott Nugent, J. C. Nugent). *Ph:* Henry Sharp. *Art dir:* Cedric Gibbons. *Ed:* Frank Sullivan, Leslie F. Wilder. *With* Louis Mann (*Adolf*), Robert Montgomery (*Nick Higginson*), Elliott Nugent (*Johnnie*), Leila Hyams (*Alma*), Clara Blandick (*Martha Wagenkampf*), Mary Doran, Francis X. Bushman Jr., Robert Mc-Wade, Dell Henderson, Henry Armetta, Jane Reid, James Donlan, Jeanne Wood, Lee Kohlmar. *Prod:* M-G-M. 9r.

WAY FOR A SAILOR (1930). *Sc. Dial:* Lawrence Stallings, W. L. River (story "Way of a Sailor" by Albert Richard Wetjen). *Add. Dial:* Charles MacArthur, Al Boasberg. *Ph:* Percy Hilburn. *Art dir:* Cedric Gibbons. *Ed:* Frank Sullivan. *With* John Gilbert (*Jack*), Wallace Beery (*Tripod*), Jim Tully (*Ginger*), Leila Hyams (*Joan*), Polly Moran (*Polly*), Doris Lloyd (*Flossy*). *Prod:* M-G-M. 9r.

PAID [GB: WITHIN THE LAW] (1930). *Sc:* Charles MacArthur, Lucien Hubbard (story "Within the Law" by Bayard Veiller). *Ph:* Charles Rosher. *Art dir:* Cedric Gibbons. *Ed:* Hugh Wynn. *With* Joan Crawford (*Mary Turner*), Robert Armstrong (*Joe Garson*), Marie Prevost (*Agnes Lynch*), Kent Douglass (*Bob Gilder*), John Miljan (*Inspector Burke*), Purnell B. Pratt, Hale Hamilton, Polly Moran, Robert Emmett O'Connor, Tyrell Davis, William Bakewell, George Cooper, Gwen Lee, Isabel Withers. *Prod:* M-G-M. 10r.

A TAILOR MADE MAN (1931). *Sc:* Edgar Allen Woolf (play by Harry James Smith). *Ph:* Albert Gilks. *Art dir:* Cedric Gibbons. *Ed:* George Hively. *With* William Haines (*John Paul Bart*),

179

Joan Crawford in PAID

Dorothy Jordan (*Tanya*), Joseph Cawthorn (*Huber*), Marjorie Rambeau (*Kitty Du Puy*), William Austin (*Jellicott*), Ian Keith, Hedda Hopper, Hale Hamilton, Henry Armetta, Walter Walker, Forrester Harvey, Joan Marsh, Martha Sleeper. *Prod:* M-G-M. 81m.

THE MAN IN POSSESSION (1931). *Sc:* Sarah Y. Mason (play by H. M. Harwood). *Add. Dial:* Sarah Y. Mason, P. G. Wodehouse. *Ph:* Oliver Marsh. *Art dir:* Cedric Gibbons. *Ed:* Ben Lewis. *With* Robert Montgomery (*Raymond Dabney*), Charlotte Greenwood (*Clara*), Irene Purcell (*Crystal Wetherby*), C. Aubrey Smith (*Mr. Dabney*), Beryl Mercer (*Mrs. Dabney*), Reginald Owen, Alan Mowbray, Maude Eburne, Forrester Harvey, Yorke Sherwood. *Prod:* M-G-M. 84m.

GET-RICH-QUICK WALLINGFORD [Alternative title: THE NEW ADVENTURES OF GET-RICH-QUICK WALLINGFORD] (1931). *Sc:* Charles MacArthur (stories by George Randolph Chester). *Ph:* Oliver Marsh. *Art dir:* Cedric Gibbons, ? *Ed:* Frank Sullivan. *With* William Haines (*Wallingford*), Leila Hyams (*Dorothy*), Ernest Torrence (*Blackie Daw*), Jimmy Durante (*Schnozzle*), Guy Kibbee (*McGonigol*), Hale Hamilton, Robert McWade, Clara Blandick, Walter Walker, Henry Armetta, Luck Beaumont. *Prod:* M-G-M. 94m.

HUDDLE [GB: THE IMPOSSIBLE LOVER] (1932). *Sc:* R. C. Johnson, A. S. Hyman (novel by Francis Wallace). *Dial:* Walter Hall Smith, C. Gardner Sullivan. *Ph:* Harold Winstrom. *Art dir:* Cedric Gibbons, ?. *Ed:* Hugh Wynn. *With* Ramon Novarro (*Tony*), Madge Evans (*Rosalie*), Una Merkel (*Thelma*), Ralph Graves (*Coach*), John Arledge (*Pidge*), Kane Richmond, Frank Albertson, Martha Sleeper, Henry Armetta, Ferike Boros, Rockliffe Fellowes, Joe Sauers [Sawyer]. *Prod:* M-G-M. 104m.

PROSPERITY (1932). *Sc:* Sylvia Thalberg, Frank Butler, Eve Greene (story by Zelda Sears). *Ph:* Leonard Smith. *Art dir:* Cedric Gibbons, ?. *Ed:* Wm. Le Vanway. *With* Marie Dressler (*Maggie Warren*), Polly Moran (*Lizzie Praskins*), Anita Page (*Helen*), Norman Foster (*John Warren*), Jacquie Lyn, Jerry Tucker, John Miljan, Charles Giblyn, Frank Darien, Henry Armetta, John Roche. *Prod:* M-G-M. 76m.

THE BARBARIAN [GB: A NIGHT IN CAIRO] (1933). *Sc:* Anita Loos, Elmer

Harris (play "The Arab" by Edgar Selwyn). *Ph:* Hal Rosson. *Art dir:* Cedric Gibbons. *Ed:* Tom Held. *Music:* Herbert Stothart. *With* Ramon Novarro (*Jamil*), Myrna Loy (*Diana*), Reginald Denny (*Gerald*), Louise Closser Hale (*Power*), C. Aubrey Smith (*Cecil*), Edward Arnold, Blanche Friderici, Marcelle Corday, Hedda Hopper, Leni Stengel. *Prod:* M-G-M. 74m. Re-make of *The Arab* (1924, Rex Ingram) and *The Arab* (1915, C. B. DeMille).

HOLD YOUR MAN (1933). *Sc:* Anita Loos, Howard Emmett Rogers (story by Loos). *Ph:* Harold G. Rosson. *Art dir:* Cedric Gibbons. *Ed:* Frank Sullivan. *With* Clark Gable (*Eddie*), Jean Harlow (*Ruby*), Stuart Erwin (*Al*), Dorothy Burgess (*Gypsy*), Muriel Kirkland (*Bertha*), Garry Owen, Barbara Barondess, Paul Hurst, Elizabeth Patterson, Theresa Harris, Blanche Friderici, George Reid, Inez Courtney, Helen Freeman. *Prod:* Sam Wood for M-G-M. 89m.

CHRISTOPHER BEAN (1933). *Sc:* Sylvia Thalberg, Larry Johnson (play by Sidney Howard). *Ph:* William Daniels. *Art dir:* Cedric Gibbons. *Ed:* Hugh Wynn. *With* Marie Dressler (*Abby*), Lionel Barrymore (*Dr. Haggett*), Helen Mack (*Susan*), Beulah Bondi (*Mrs. Haggett*), Russell Hardie (*Warren*), Jean Hersholt, H. B. Warner, Helen Shipman, George Coulouris, Ellen Lowe. *Prod:* Harry Rapf for M-G-M. 87m. Featurette re-make in 1957, directed by Lewis Allen. Some sources give HER SWEETHEART, CHRISTOPHER BEAN as an alternative title for Wood's film.

STAMBOUL QUEST (1934). *Sc:* Herman Mankiewicz (story by Leo Birin-

ski). *Ph:* James Wong Howe. *Art dir:* Cedric Gibbons, Stan Rogers. *Ed:* Hugh Wynn. *With* Myrna Loy (*Annemarie*), George Brent (*Beall*), Lionel Atwill (*Von Sturm*), C. Henry Gordon (*Ali Bey*), Rudolph Amendt (*Karl*), Mischa Auer. *Prod:* M-G-M. 90m.

LET 'EM HAVE IT (GB: FALSE FACES) (1935). *Sc:* Joseph M. March, Elmer Harris (from own story). *Ph:* J. Peverell Marley, Robert Planck. *Ed:* Grant Whytock. *With* Richard Arlen (*Mal Stevens*), Virginia Bruce (*Eleanor Spencer*), Alice Brady (*Aunt Ethel*), Bruce Cabot (*Joe Keefer*), Harvey Stephens (*Van Rensseler*), Eric Linden, Joyce Compton, Gordon Jones, J. Farrell MacDonald, Bodil Rosing, Paul Stanton, Robert E. O'Connor, Hale Hamilton, Dorothy Appleby, Barbara Pepper, Mathew Betz, Paul Fix, Harry Woods, Clyde Dillson, Donald Kirke, Eugene Strong, Christian Rub, Eleanor Wesselhoeft, Wesley Barry, Ian MacLaren, Joseph King, George Pauncefort, Clarence Wilson, Landers Stevens, Matty Fain, Katherine Clare Ward, Sidney Bracey. *Prod:* Edward Small for Reliance Pictures. *Dist:* United Artists. 95m.

A NIGHT AT THE OPERA (1935). *Sc:* George S. Kaufman, Morrie Ryskind (story by James Kevin McGuinness). *Add. material:* Al Boasberg. *Ph:* Merritt B. Gerstad. *Art dir:* Cedric Gibbons, Ben Carre. *Set dec:* Edwin B. Willis. *Ed:* Wm. Le Vanway. *Music:* Herbert Stothart. *With* Groucho Marx (*Otis B. Driftwood*), Harpo Marx (*Tomasso*), Chico Marx (*Fiorello*), Margaret Dumont (*Mrs. Claypool*), Siegfried Rumann (*Herman Gottlieb*), Kitty Carlisle, Allan Jones, Walter Woolf King, Edward

Keane, Robert Emmett O'Connor, Lorraine Bridges. *Prod:* Irving Thalberg for M-G-M. 93m.

WHIPSAW (1936). *Sc:* Howard Emmett Rogers (story by James Edward Grant). *Ph:* James Wong Howe. *Art dir:* Cedric Gibbons, William Horning. *Sets:* Edwin B. Willis. *Ed:* Basil Wrangell. *Music:* William Axt. *With* Myrna Loy (*Vivian Palmer*), Spencer Tracy (*Ross McBride*), Harvey Stephens (*Ed Dexter*), William Harrigan (*Doc Evans*), Clay Clement (*Harry Ames*), George Renavent, Robert Warwick, John Qualen, Robert Gleckler, Paul Stanton, Wade Boteler, Don Rowan, Irene Franklin, Lillian Leighton, J. Anthony Hughes, William Ingersoll, Halliwell Hobbes, Charles Irwin. *Prod:* Harry Rapf for M-G-M. 83m.

THE UNGUARDED HOUR (1936). *Sc:* Howard Emmett Rogers, Leon Gordon (play by Ladislaus Fodor). *Ph:* James Van Trees. *Art dir:* Cedric Gibbons. *Ed:* Frank Hull. *Music:* William Axt. *With* Loretta Young (*Lady Helen Dearden*), Franchot Tone (*Sir Alan Dearden*), Lewis Stone (*General Lawrence*), Roland Young (*Bunny*), Jessie Ralph (*Lady Hathaway*), Dudley Digges, Henry Daniell, Robert Grieg, E. E. Clive, Wallis Clark, John Buckler, Aileen Pringle. *Prod:* Lawrence Weingarten for M-G-M. 86m.

A DAY AT THE RACES (1937). *Sc:* George Seaton, Robert Pirosh, George Oppenheimer (story by Seaton and Pirosh). *Ph:* Joseph Ruttenberg. *Art dir:* Cedric Gibbons, Stan Rogers. *Sets:* Edwin B. Willis. *Ed:* Frank E. Hull. *Music:* Franz Waxman. *With* Groucho Marx (*Dr. Hugo Z. Hackenbush*), Harpo Marx (*Stuffy*), Chico Marx (*Toni*), Margaret Dumont (*Mrs. Emily Upjohn*), Siegfried Rumann (*Dr. Leopold X. Steinberg*), Allan Jones, Maureen O'Sullivan, Douglas Dumbrille, Leonard Ceeley, Esther Muir, Robert Middlemass, Vivien Fay, Dennis O'Keefe, Ivie Anderson and the Crinoline Choir [including Dorothy Dandridge]. *Prod:* Irving Thalberg, Sam Wood for M-G-M. 109m.

NAVY BLUE AND GOLD (1937).

Wood with James Stewart during filming of NAVY BLUE AND GOLD

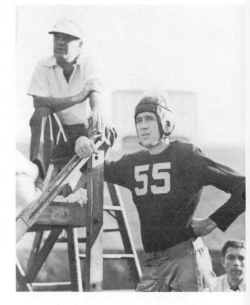

Sc: George Bruce (from his novel). *Ph:* John Seitz. *Art dir:* Cedric Gibbons. *Ed:* Robert J. Kern. *Montage:* John Hoffman. *Music:* Edward Ward. *With* James Stewart (*"Truck" Cross*), Robert Young (*Roger Ash*), Lionel Barrymore (*Capt. "Skinny" Dawes*), Florence Rice (*Patricia Gates*), Billie Burke (*Mrs. Gates*), Tom Brown, Paul Kelly, Barnett Parker, Samuel S. Hinds, Frank Albertson, Minor Watson, Philip Terry, Robert Middlemass, Charles Waldron, Pat Flaherty, Stanley Morner [later Dennis Morgan], K. T. Stevens, Matt McHugh, Ted Pearson. *Prod:* Sam Zimbalist for M-G-M. 94m.

MADAME X (1937). *Sc:* John Meehan (play by Alexandre Bisson). *Ph:* John Seitz. *Art dir:* Cedric Gibbons. *Ed:* Frank E. Hull. *Music:* David Snell. *With* Gladys George (*Jacqueline Fleuriot*), Warren William (*Bernard Fleuriot*), John Beal (*Raymond Fleuriot*), Reginald Owen (*Maurice Dourel*), William Henry (*Hugh Fairman, Jr.*), Henry Daniell, Philip Reed, Lynne Carver, Emma Dunn, Ruth Hussey, Luis Alberni, George Zucco, Cora Witherspoon, Jonathan Hale, Adia Kuznetzoff. *Prod:* James Kevin McGuinness for M-G-M. 72m. Other versions filmed in 1916; 1920 (*d.* Frank Lloyd), 1929 (*d.* Lionel Barrymore) and 1965 (*d.* David Lowell Rich).

LORD JEFF (GB: THE BOY FROM BARNADO'S) (1938). *Sc:* James Kevin McGuinness (story by Bradford Ropes, Val Burton, Andre Bohem). *Ph:* John Seitz. *Art dir:* Cedric Gibbons. *Ed:* Frank E. Hull. *Music:* Edward Ward. *With* Freddie Bartholomew (*Geoffrey Braemer*), Mickey Rooney (*Terry O'Mul-*vaney), Charles Coburn (*Capt. Briggs*), Herbert Mundin (*"Crusty" Jelks*), Terry Kilburn (*Albert Baker*), Gale Sondergaard, Peter Lawford, Walter Tetley, Peter Ellis, George Zucco, Matthew Boulton, John Burton, Emma Dunn, Monty Woolley, Gilbert Emery, Charles Irwin, Walter Kingsford. *Prod:* Sam Wood, Frank Davis for M-G-M. 85m.

STABLEMATES (1938). *Sc:* Leonard Praskins, Richard Maibaum (story by William Thiele, Reginald Owen). *Ph:* John Seitz. *Art dir:* Cedric Gibbons. *Ed:* W. Dan Hayes. *Music:* Edward Ward. *With* Wallace Beery (*Tom Terry*), Mickey Rooney (*Mickey*), Arthur Hohl (*Mr. Gale*), Margaret Hamilton (*Beulah Flanders*), Minor Watson (*Barney Donovan*), Marjorie Gateson, Oscar O'Shea, Jennie Morris, Sam McDaniel. *Prod:* Harry Rapf for M-G-M. 89m.

RAFFLES (1939). *Sc:* John Van Druten, Sidney Howard (novel "The Amateur Cracksman" by E. W. Hornung). *Ph:* Gregg Toland. *Ed:* Sherman Todd. *Music:* Victor Young. *With* David Niven (*Raffles*), Olivia de Havilland (*Gwen*), Dame May Whitty (*Lady Melrose*), Dudley Digges (*Mackenzie*), Douglas Walton (*Bunny*), Lionel Pape, Peter Godfrey, E. E. Clive, Margaret Seddon, Gilbert Emery, Hilda Plowright, Vesey O'Davoren, George Cathrey, Keith Hitchcock. *Prod:* Samuel Goldwyn. 71m. Other versions include 1904 (*d.* J. Stuart Blackton); 1925 (*d.* King Baggot) and 1930 (*d.* Harry D'Arrast, George Fitzmaurice).

GOODBYE, MR. CHIPS (1939). *Sc:* R. C. Sherriff, Claudine West, Eric Maschwitz (novel by James Hilton). *Ph:* F. A. Young. *Ed:* Charles Frend.

Music: Louis Levy. *With* Robert Donat (*Mr. Chips*), Greer Garson (*Katherine*), Terry Kilburn (*John Colley/Peter Colley 1/Peter Colley 2/Peter Colley 3*), John Mills (*Peter Colley as a young man*), Paul von Hernreid [later Paul Henreid] (*Staefel*), Judith Furse, Lyn Harding, Milton Rosmer, Frederick Leister, Louise Hampton, Austin Trevor, David Tree, Edmond Breon, Jill Furse, Scott Sunderland, Cyril Raymond, John Longden, Guy Middleton, Michael Shepley, Nigel Stock. *Prod:* Victor Saville for M-G-M. 114m. Re-made in 1970 by Herbert Ross.

OUR TOWN (1940). *Sc:* Thornton Wilder, Frank Craven, Harry Chandlee (play by Wilder). *Ph:* Bert Glennon. *Art dir:* William Cameron Menzies, Harry Horner. *Ed:* Sherman Todd. *Music:* Aaron Copland. *With* William Holden (*George Gibbs*), Martha Scott (*Emily Webb*), Fay Bainter (*Mrs. Gibbs*), Beulah Bondi (*Mrs. Webb*), Thomas Mitchell (*Dr. Gibbs*), Guy Kibbee, Stuart Erwin, Frank Craven, Doro Merande, Philip Wood, Ruth Toby, Douglas Gardiner, Arthur Allen, Charles Trowbridge, Spencer Charters, Dix Davis, Tim Davis. *Prod:* Sol Lesser for Sol Lesser Productions. *Dist:* United Artists. 90m.

KITTY FOYLE (1940). *Sc:* Dalton Trumbo, Donald Ogden Stewart (story by Christopher Morley). *Ph:* Robert De Grasse. *Art dir:* Van Nest Polglase. *Ed:* Henry Berman. *Music:* Roy Webb. *With* Ginger Rogers (*Kitty Foyle*), Dennis Morgan (*Wyn Strafford*), Eduardo Ciannelli (*Giono*), James Craig (*Mark*), Ernest Cossart (*Pop*), Gladys Cooper, Odette Myrtil, Mary Treen, K. T. Stevens, Walter Kingsford, Cecil Cunningham, Nella Walker, Edward Fielding, Kay Linaker, Richard Nichols, Florence Bates. *Prod:* David Hempstead, Harry F. Edington for RKO. 108m.

RANGERS OF FORTUNE (1940). *Sc:* Frank Butler. *Ph:* Theodor Sparkuhl. *Art dir:* Hans Dreier, Robert Usher. *Ed:* Eda Warren. *Music:* Frederick Hollander. *With* Fred MacMurray (*Gil Farra*), Albert Dekker (*Col. Bird*), Gilbert Roland (*Sierra*), Patricia Morison (*Sharon*), Betty Brewer (*Squib*), Joseph Schildkraut, Dick Foran, Arthur Allen, Bernard Nedell, Brandon Tynan, Minor Watson, Rosa Turich. *Prod:* Dale Van Every for Paramount. 80m.

THE DEVIL AND MISS JONES (1941). *Sc:* Norman Krasna (from his story). *Ph:* Harry Stradling. *Art dir:* William Cameron Menzies. *Ed:* Sherman Todd. *Music:* Roy Webb. *With* Jean Arthur (*Mary*), Robert Cummings (*Joe*), Charles Coburn (*Merrick*), Edmund Gwenn (*Hooper*), Spring Byington (*Elizabeth*), S. Z. Sakall, William Demarest, Walter Kingsford, Edwin Maxwell, Richard Carle, Charles Waldron, Montagu Love, Edward McNamara, Robert Emmett Keane, Florence Bates, Charles Irwin, Matt McHugh, Julie Warren, Ilene Brewer, Regis Toomey, Pat Moriarty, George Watts. *Prod:* Frank Ross, Norman Krasna for RKO. 90m.

KINGS ROW (1942). *Sc:* Casey Robinson (novel by Henry Bellamann). *Ph:* James Wong Howe. *Art dir:* Carl Jules Weyl. *Ed:* Ralph Dawson. *Music:* Erich Wolfgang Korngold. *With* Ann Sheridan (*Randy Monaghan*), Robert Cummings (*Parris Mitchell*), Ronald Reagan (*Drake*

McHugh), Betty Field (*Cassandra Tower*), Charles Coburn (*Dr. Henry Gordon*), Claude Rains (*Dr. Alexander Tower*), Judith Anderson, Nancy Coleman, Kaaren Verne, Maria Ouspenskaya, Harry Davenport, Ernest Cossart, Ilka Gruning, Pat Moriarty, Minor Watson, Ludwig Stossel, Erwin Kaiser, Egon Brecher, Ann E. Todd, Scotty Beckett, Douglas Croft, Mary Thomas, Julie Warren, Mary Scott, Joan Duval, Thomas W. Ross. *Prod:* Hal B. Wallis. *Assoc. Prod:* David Lewis for Warner Bros. 130m.

THE PRIDE OF THE YANKEES (1942). *Sc:* Herman J. Mankiewicz, Jo Swerling (story by Paul Gallico). *Ph:* Rudolph Mate. *Art dir:* Perry Ferguson. *Ed:* Daniel Mandell. *Music:* Leigh Harline. *With* Gary Cooper (*Lou Gehrig*), Teresa Wright (*Eleanor Gehrig*), Walter Brennan (*Sam Blake*), Dan Duryea (*Hank Hanneman*), Babe Ruth (*Himself*), Elsa Janssen, Ludwig Stossel, Virginia Gilmore, Bill Dickey, Ernie Adams, Pierre Watkin, Harry Harvey, Robert W. Meusel, Mark Koenig, Bill Stern, Addison Richards, Hardie Albright, Edward Fielding, George Lessey, Edgar Barrier, Douglas Croft, Gene Collins, David Holt, Veloz and Yolanda, Ray Noble and his Orchestra, Vaughan Glaser, Frank Faylen, Lane Chandler, George Offerman Jr., David Manley, Anita Bolster, Jimmy Valentine, Spencer Charters, Sarah Padden, Bernard Zaneville [later Dane Clark], Tom Neal, Lorna Dunn, Emory Parnell, Dorothy Vaughan, Patsy O'Byrne, Matt McHugh, William Chaney, Pat Flaherty, Francis Sayles. *Prod:* Sam Goldwyn for RKO. 128m.

FOR WHOM THE BELL TOLLS (1943). *Sc:* Dudley Nichols (novel by Hemingway). *Ph:* Ray Rennahan. *Prod. Designer:* William Cameron Menzies. *Art dir:* Hans Dreier, Haldane Douglas. *Ed:* Sherman Todd, John Link. *Music:* Victor Young. *With* Gary Cooper (*Robert Jordan*), Ingrid Bergman (*Maria*), Akim Tamiroff (*Pablo*), Arturo de Cordova (*Agustin*), Vladimir Sokoloff (*Anselmo*), Mikhail Rasumny, Fortunio Bonanova, Eric Feldary, Victor Varconi, Joseph Calleia, Katina Paxinou, Lilo Yarson, Alexander Granach, Adia Kuznetzoff, Leonid Snegoff, Leo Bulgakov, Duncan Renaldo, George Coulouris, Frank Puglia, Pedro de Cordoba, Michael Visaroff, Konstantin Shayne, Martin Garralaga, Jean Del Val, Jack Mylong, Feodor Chaliapin, Mayo Newball, Michael Dalmatoff, Antonio Vidal, Robert Tafur, Armand Roland, Trini Varela,

Wood on location for FOR WHOM THE BELL TOLLS, with writer Dudley Nichols and actor Joseph Calleia

Dick Botiller, Franco Corsaro, Frank Lackteen, George Sorel, John Bleifer, Harry Cording, William Edmunds, Yakima Canutt, Tito Renaldo, Maxine Ardell, Marjorie Deanne, Yvonne De Carlo, Alice Kirby, Marcella Phillips, Lynda Grey, Christopher King, Louise La Planche, Alberto Morin, Pedro Regas, Soledad Jiminez, Luis Rojas, Manuel Paris, Jose Tortosa, Ernesto Morelli, Manuel Lopez. *Prod:* Sam Wood for Paramount. 168m.

CASANOVA BROWN (1944). *Sc:* Nunnally Johnson (play "The Little Accident" by Floyd Dell, Thomas Mitchell). *Ph:* John Seitz. *Art dir:* Perry Ferguson. *Ed:* Thomas Neff. *Music:* Arthur Lange. *With* Gary Cooper (*Casanova Brown*), Teresa Wright (*Isabel Drury*), Frank Morgan (*Mr. Ferris*), Patricia Collinge (*Mrs. Drury*), Edmond Breon (*Mr. Drury*), Anita Louise, Jill Esmond, Isabel Elsom, Mary Treen, Emory Parnell, Halliwell Hobbes, Larry Joe Olsen,

Gary Cooper and Teresa Wright in CASANOVA BROWN

Byron Foulger, Sarah Padden, Grady Sutton, Eloise Hardt, Frederick Burton, Robert Dudley, Isabel Le Mal, Florence Lake, Ann Evans, Frances Morris, Nell Craig, Lane Chandler, Kay Deslys, Ottiola Nesmith, Lorna Dunn, Kelly Flint, Dorothy Tree, Isabel Withers, Irving Bacon, James Burke, Francis Sayles, Phil Tead, Snub Pollard, Grace Cunard, Verna Kornman, Anna Luther, Marian Gray, Sada Simmons, Lelah Tyler, Cecil Stewart, Helen St. Rayner, Stewart Garner, Mary Young, John Brown, Jack Gargan, Billy Chapin. *Prod:* Nunnally Johnson for International Pictures. *Dist:* RKO. 99m.

SARATOGA TRUNK (1945). [Filmed in 1943]. *Sc:* Casey Robinson (novel by Edna Ferber). *Ph:* Ernest Haller. *Art dir:* Carl Jules Weyl. *Ed:* Ralph Dawson. *Music:* Max Steiner. *With* Gary Cooper (*Col. Clint Maroon*), Ingrid Bergman (*Clio Dulaine*), Flora Robson (*Angelique Buiton*), Jerry Austin (*Cupidon*), John Warburton (*Bartholomew Van Stead*), Florence Bates, Curt Bois, John Abbott, Ethel Griffies, Marla Shelton, Helen Freeman, Sophie Huxley, Fred Essler, Louis Payne, Sarah Edwards, Jacqueline De Witt, Minor Watson, Adrienne D'Ambricourt, J. Lewis Johnson, Libby Taylor, Lillian Yorke, Geneva Williams, Ruby Dandridge, Paul Bryant, Shelby Bacon, Peter Cusanelli, George Humbert, Bertha Woolford, George Reed, Amelia Liggett, George Beranger, John Sylvester, Edmond Breon, William B. Davidson, Edward Fielding, Thurston Hall, Alice Fleming, Ralph Dunn, Lane Chandler, Glenn Strange, Chester Clute, Theodore Von Eltz, Monte Blue, Franklyn Farnum, Bob

Reeves, Al Ferguson, Hank Bell, Dick Elliott. *Prod:* Hal B. Wallis for Warner Bros. 135m.

GUEST WIFE (1945). *Sc:* John Klorer, Bruce Manning. *Ph:* Joseph Valentine. *Art dir:* Lionel Bates. *Ed:* William V. Morgan. *Music:* Daniele Amfitheatrof. *With* Claudette Colbert (*Mary*), Don Ameche (*Joe*), Richard Foran (*Chris*), Charles Dingle (*Worth*), Grant Mitchell (*Detective*), Wilma Francis, Hal K. Dawson, Chester Clute, Irving Bacon, Edward Fielding. *Prod:* Jack H. Skirball for United Artists. 90m.

HEARTBEAT (1946). *Sc:* Morrie Ryskind (based on screenplay for "Battement de Coeur" [1939, *d.* Henri Decoin] by Hans Wilhelm, Max Kolpe and Rowland Leigh [Michel Duran]). *Ph:* Joseph Valentine. *Art dir:* Lionel Banks. *Ed:* Roland Gross. *Music:* Paul Misraki. *With* Ginger Rogers (*Arlette*), Jean-Pierre Aumont (*Pierre*), Adolphe Menjou (*Ambassador*), Basil Rathbone (*Professor Aristide*), Eduardo Ciannelli (*Baron Dvorak*), Henry Stephenson, Melville Cooper, Mikhail Rasumny, Mona Maris. *Prod:* Robert Hakim, Raymond Hakim for RKO. 101m.

IVY (1947). *Sc:* Charles Bennett (novel "The Story of Ivy" by Marie Belloc Lowndes). *Ph:* Russell Metty. *Art dir:* Richard H. Reidel. *Ed:* Ralph Dawson. *Music:* Daniele Amfitheatroff. *With* Joan Fontaine (*Ivy*), Patric Knowles (*Roger*), Herbert Marshall (*Miles Rushworth*), Richard Ney (*Jarvis Lexton*), Sir Cedric Hardwicke (*Inspector Orpington*), Lucile Watson, Sara Allgood, Henry Stephenson, Rosalind Ivan, Lilian Fontaine, Molly Lamont, Una O'Connor, Isobel Elsom, Alan Napier, Paul Cavanagh, Sir Charles Mendl, Gavin Muir, Mary Forbes. *Prod:* Sam Wood, William Cameron Menzies for Universal-International. 99m.

COMMAND DECISION (1949). *Sc:* William R. Laidlaw, George Froeschel (play by William Wister Haines). *Ph:* Harold Rosson. *Art dir:* Cedric Gibbons, Urie McLeary. *Ed:* Harold F. Kress. *Music:* Miklos Rozsa. *With* Clark Gable (*Brig. General K. C. Dennis*), Walter Pidgeon (*Major General Roland Goodlow Kane*), Van Johnson (*Tech. Sgt. Immanuel T. Evans*), Brian Donlevy (*Brig. General Clifton I. Garnett*), Charles Bickford (*Elmer Brockhurst*), John Hodiak, Edward Arnold, Marshall Thompson, Richard Quine, Cameron Mitchell, Clinton Sundberg, Ray Collins, Warner Anderson, John McIntire, Moroni Olsen, John Ridgely, Michael Steele, Edward Earle, Mack Williams, James Millican. *Prod:* Sidney Franklin for M-G-M. 112m.

THE STRATTON STORY (1949). *Sc:* Douglas Morrow, Guy Trosper (story by Morrow). *Ph:* Harold Rosson. *Art dir:* Cedric Gibbons, Paul Groesse. *Ed:* Ben Lewis. *Music:* Adolphe Deutsch. *With* James Stewart (*Monty Stratton*), June Allyson (*Ethel*), Frank Morgan (*Barney Wile*), Agnes Moorehead (*Ma Stratton*), Bill Williams (*Eddie Dibson*), Bruce Cowling, Cliff Clarke, Mary Lawrence, Dean White, Robert Gist, Gene Beardon, Bill Dickey, Jimmy Dykes, Mervyn Shea. *Prod:* Jack Cummings for M-G-M. 106m.

AMBUSH (1950). *Sc:* Marguerite Roberts (story by Luke Short). *Ph:* Harold Lipstein. *Art dir:* Cedric Gibbons, Malcolm Brown. *Ed:* Ben Lewis. *Music:*

Rudolph G. Kopp. *With* Robert Taylor (*Ward Kinsman*), John Hodiak (*Capt. Ben Lorrison*), Arlene Dahl (*Ann Duverall*), Don Taylor (*Lieut. Linus Delaney*), Jean Hagen (*Martha Conovan*), John McIntire, Bruce Cowling, Leon Ames, Pat Moriarty, Charles Stevens, Chief Thundercloud, Ray Teal, Robin Short, Richard Bailey. *Prod:* Armand Deutsch for M-G-M. **89m.**

Wood also directed several scenes (see text), uncredited, in *Gone with the Wind* (1939, Victor Fleming, George Cukor, Leslie Howard, David O. Selznick, William A. Wellman *et al*).

He also supervised a 1943 propaganda documentary entitled *The Land Is Bright,* and produced *Address Unknown* (1944, William Cameron Menzies).

Plot synopses have been omitted from the filmography, since they are fully covered in the text. The character names for the silent films have been taken from the American Film Institute Catalogue of Films made between 1920-30, but in some instances (marked °) they differ from those given in a reliable British periodical. Additional material for the filmography prepared by Kingsley Canham, with the assistance of Jean Canham and Robert Holton.

°   °   °

Wood with George K. Arthur and Karl Dane while making ROOKIES. Opposite: Wood with Ginger Rogers

Index